明长城

THE MING GREAT WALL

国家文物局　编　　Edited by State Administration of Cultural Heritage

文物出版社

Cultural Relics Press

责任编辑　李克能
　　　　　张广然
　　　　　冯冬梅
封面设计　张希广
英文翻译　丁晓雷
责任印制　张道奇
责任校对　安倩敏
　　　　　陈　婧

图书在版编目（CIP）数据

明长城 / 国家文物局编. —— 北京：文物出版社，
2012.8

　　ISBN 978-7-5010-3455-0

　　Ⅰ．①明… Ⅱ．①国… Ⅲ．①长城－调查报告
－中国－明代 Ⅳ．①K928.77

　　中国版本图书馆CIP数据核字（2012）第103203号

明长城

编　　者　国家文物局
出版发行　文物出版社
社　　址　北京市东直门内北小街 2 号楼
邮政编码　100007
网　　址　www.wenwu.com
邮　　箱　web@wenwu.com
制版印刷　北京图文天地制版印刷有限公司
经　　销　新华书店
开　　本　889×1194毫米　1/16
印　　张　22.75
版　　次　2012年8月第1版
印　　次　2012年8月第1次印刷
书　　号　ISBN　978-7-5010-3455-0
定　　价　360.00元

目　录
CONTENTS

序

　　长城，是世界上规模、体量最大的人工构筑物，是中华民族勤劳智慧的结晶，是中国劳动人民创造的工程奇迹，是中华文明的突出见证。长城建筑时间之长、分布地域之广、影响力之大，是其他任何文物都无法比拟的，它已成为中华民族伟大精神的象征。长城整体及其重要节点、段落等相继被国务院公布为全国重点文物保护单位，实施依法保护。1987年，长城作为"全人类最令人震惊的文化遗产之一"，因其独特的历史、艺术和科学价值被整体列入《世界遗产名录》，成为我国首批世界文化遗产。

　　长城由墙体、敌台、马面、烽火台、关、堡等多种防御工事组成，是一个规模庞大的军事防御工程体系，以其复杂和艰苦的施工、严密而科学的战略布局、宏伟而坚固的结构闻名于世。长城始建于春秋战国时期，此后，汉、晋、北魏、东魏、西魏、北齐、北周、隋、唐、宋、辽、金、元、明等十多个朝代，都不同规模地修筑过长城。历代长城分布于我国的北京、天津、河北、山西、内蒙古、辽宁、吉林、黑龙江、山东、河南、湖北、陕西、甘肃、青海、宁夏、新疆16个省、自治区、直辖市。

　　长城在修筑过程中巧妙利用自然山体、河流，坚持"因地制宜、用险置塞"的理念，根据不同地理区域特点，采用不同材质构建多样的建筑结构，充分体现了古代人类社会修筑技术的绝妙智慧。长城与周边自然、人文环境完美结合，具有突出的建筑艺术和美学价值，是具有显著文化景观特征的巨型线性文化遗产。长城总体布局及各构成要素保存完整，其位置、工艺、形状、结构基本保存了历史原貌，具有极高的真实性和完整性。然而，由于经历了漫长的历史时期，长城仍不可避免地面临着自然侵蚀以及旅游开发、城市发展等人为因素带来的威胁。

　　长城保护工作得到中国党和政府的高度重视，党中央、国务院领导同志多次对长城保护工作做出重要批示，要求摸清长城家底，切实做好长城保护工作。为妥善保护这一极为珍贵的文化遗产，国家文物局发布了《"长城保护工程（2005～2014年）"总体工作方案》，并于2006年2月正式启动长城保护工程，争取用较短的时间摸清长城家底、建立健全相关法规制度、理顺管理体制，在统一规划的指导下，科学安排长城保护维修、合理利用等工作，并依法加强监管，从根本上遏制对长城的破坏，为长城保护管理工作的良性发展打下坚实基础。

　　2006年，国务院颁布《长城保护条例》，这是我国政府首次为单项文化遗产开展保护立法工作，标志着长城保护法律体系的初步建立。与此同时，在国家文物局统一部署和组织指导下，各地相继启动了长城资源调查、长城档案及信息系统建设、长城保护规划编制、长城重点段落及节点保护修缮等工作。从整体上看，通过长城沿线各省、自治区、直辖市文物工作者的共同努力，长城保护管理和科学研究工作正在得到显著加强。2009年，国家文物局和国家测绘局合作开展的明长城资源调查工作全部完成，并向社会公布了明长城长度数据8851.8千米。目前，已全面完成其他各时代长城的田野调查，进入资料数据汇总阶段，长城各时代资源调查成果汇集工作也正在有序推进。通过长城资源调查工作，全面、准确、详尽地掌握了长城的规模、分布、构成、走向、时代属性及保存现状，为科学开展长城保护、修缮及展示利用工作提供了科学依据。此外，我国还重点加大了长城保护资金投入，相继实施并完成了山海关段、嘉峪关段等长城重要段落的保护工程，妥善保护了长城本体及周边环境景观。

我们相信，随着长城保护工程的不断推进，通过长城沿线文物工作者的不懈努力，必将有更多的长城段落、节点及周边环境景观得到保护和改善，切实保护和传承长城突出的普遍价值及真实性、完整性，最终实现长城保护管理工作的良性发展。

为记录我国长城保护工作进展情况，增强全社会保护长城的意识，宣传长城保护各项成果，促进长城保护工作成果惠及社会大众，国家文物局组织长城沿线各省、自治区、直辖市文物行政部门及相关科研机构共同编辑出版《长城保护工程丛书》。本丛书将包括长城资源调查报告集、长城保护修缮工程报告集、各时代长城专题研究报告集、长城信息系统建设报告等系列丛书，并将随着长城保护工程的开展陆续面世。我们希望本丛书的编辑出版工作将对长城保护工作产生积极的作用。

同时，我们也希望通过本套丛书的出版，向战斗在我国长城保护工程第一线的全体文物工作者致以最崇高的敬意！

国家文物局

二○一○年十二月

Preface

The Great Wall of China is the largest artificial construction on the world, the crystal of the industriousness and wisdom of the Chinese people, the engineering wonder created by Chinese laboring people and the outstanding evidence of Chinese Civilization. The time span of the construction, the distribution scope and the influence of the Great Wall are all peerless among the historic and cultural monuments in China and it has been the symbol of the great spirit of Chinese nationality. The important landmarks and sections of the Great Wall have been successively proclaimed by the State Council as the historic and cultural sites under state protection. In 1987, as one of the astonishing cultural heritages of the mankind, the Great Wall as a whole was listed as the World Heritage and became one of the first set of the world heritages of China.

Consisting of the walls, watchtowers, bastions, beacon towers, passes and fortresses, the Great Wall was a large-scale military fortification system worldly famous for its complex and audacious construction, tight and scientific strategic arrangement and magnificent and strong structure. The earliest Great Wall was built in the Spring-and-Autumn to the Warring-States Periods. Since then, the Han, Western Jin, Northern Wei, Eastern Wei, Western Wei, Northern Qi, Northern Zhou, Sui, Tang, Song, Liao, Jin, Yuan and Ming Dynasties all have built the Great Wall in various scales. The Great Walls of these periods are distributed in Beijing, Tianjin, Hebei, Shanxi, Inner Mongolia, Liaoning, Jilin, Heilongjiang, Shandong, Henan, Hubei, Shaanxi, Gansu, Qinghai, Ningxia, Xinjiang and other provinces, autonomous regions, and municipalities.

The construction of the Great Wall was skillfully taking advantages of the natural terrains such as the mountains and rivers according to the idea of "using the best of local conditions and setting the forts at the perilous topographies", and applying various types of defense facilities with local available materials, all of which reflected the intelligent military architects in ancient times. The Great Wall perfectly integrated with the surrounding natural and artificial environments and showing the splendid architectural artistic and aesthetic values is the huge linear cultural heritage with obvious characteristics of cultural vista. The general layout and the heritage elements are all well preserved, their locations, techniques, forms and structures are basically protected as they were in history, so the Great Wall has high authenticity and completeness. However, due to the long history, the Great Wall is inevitably threatened by the natural weathering and the developments of tourism and urbanism.

The protection of the Great Wall is highly emphasized by the Party and the Government; the leaders of the Central Committee of CPC and the State Council have given many times of important directions to the protection of the Great Wall and required the details of the status of the Great Wall to be surveyed and the stable protection plans to be designed. To suitably protect this invaluable cultural heritage, State Administration of Cultural Heritage issued the General Plan for the Great Wall Protection Project (2005-2014) and officially started the Great Wall Protection Project in February 2006, in order to make clear the status of the Great Wall, establish and improve the related rules, regulations and management system, scientifically arrange the protection and amendment work and rational utilization of the Great Wall under the direction of the unified plan, and strengthen the supervision and management to get rid of the spoiling of the Great Wall and lay down a firm foundation for the positive development of the protection and management of the Great Wall.

In 2006, the State Council issued the Regulation on the Protection of Great Wall, which is the first regulation issued by the central government for the protection of a single cultural heritage, symbolizing the preliminary establishment of the legal system for the protection of the Great Wall. Meanwhile, under the unified arrangement and organization of the State Administration of Cultural Heritage, the local governments of the relevant regions successively started the Great Wall resource survey, the Great Wall archive and information system construction, the Great Wall Protection plan designation, the preservations and amendments of the key sections and landmarks, and so on. Seen as a whole, the protection, management and researches of the Great Wall are greatly improved through the efforts of the provinces, autonomous regions and municipalities in which the parts of the Great Wall are located. In 2009, State Administration of Cultural Heritage and National Administration of Surveying, Mapping and Geoinformation completed the cooperative Investigation and Measurement of the Ming Great Wall Resources and published the datum of the length of the Ming Great Wall—8851.8 km; to date, the onsite investigations of the Great Walls of other periods have been finished and the data compilation has been started; the Great Wall resource investigations and result processions are also conducted in good order. Through the Great Wall resource investigations, the scales, distributions, compositions, courses, temporal attributions and preservation statuses of the Great Walls are comprehensively, accurately and thoroughly grasped and the scientific evidences are provided for the scientific preservation, amendment, display and utilization of the Great Wall. In addition, the Government increased the investment of the Great Wall protection and completed the preservation projects of some important sections such as the Shanhaiguan Pass and Jiayuguan Pass and so on, and suitably protected the Great Wall and the environmental landscapes.

We believe that along with the progression of the Great Wall Protection Project and through the relentless efforts of the cultural heritage workers on the Great Wall, there are going to be more and more Great Wall sections, landmarks and environmental landscapes protected and bettered, the special and exceptional value, the authenticity and completeness of the Great Wall are going to be handed down and the protection and management of the Great Wall are going to be positively developed.

To record the development of the Great Wall Protection Project, enhance the social idea of protecting the Great Wall and publicizing the achievements of the Great Wall protection in order to share them to the public, the State Administration of Cultural Heritage organizes the cultural relics management agencies and relevant research institutions of the provinces, autonomous regions and municipalities in which the sections of the Great Wall are located to edit and publish this Series on the Great Wall Protection Project. This series will include the collection of the reports on the Great Wall resource investigations, the reports on the Great Wall protection and amendment projects, the monographs on the Great Walls of all of the periods, the Great Wall information system construction reports, and other subseries, which will be published successively with the development of the Great Wall Protection Project. We hope that the editing and publishing of this series will play a good role in the protection of the Great Wall.

Meanwhile, we hope to pay the highest respect to the cultural heritage workers fighting on the frontiers of the Great Wall protection by the publishing of this series!

State Administration of Cultural Heritage
December 2010

明长城资源调查与收获

柴晓明　杨招君

长城到底有多长？是一个十分浅显的问题，因为每个中国人，甚至全世界许多人都知道中国有"万里"长城。这又是一个让许多专业人士纠结不已的心病，自从长城出现在中华大地之日起，两千多年来从没有人知道确切答案。近年来，长城仍然因自然和人为原因遭到侵蚀和破坏，更让有识之士和社会公众忧心忡忡。针对长城保护问题，2005年初，国家文物局制定了《"长城保护工程（2005～2014年）"总体工作方案》，得到国务院领导同意。该方案明确近期长城保护工作要达到的目标是：争取用较短的时间摸清长城家底、建立健全相关法规制度、理顺管理体制，在统一规划的指导下，科学安排长城保护维修、合理利用等工作，并依法加强监管，从根本上遏制对长城的破坏，为长城保护管理工作的良性发展打下坚实基础。其中，摸清长城"家底"——长城资源调查被列为"长城保护工程"的第一项，也是最基础的首要任务。明长城资源调查是整个长城资源调查工作的第一阶段。目前，明长城资源调查各项工作基本完成，成果丰硕。

一、科学统筹部署，合作开拓创新

长城体系庞大、遗存丰富、所处环境十分复杂，是世界上规模最大、保护难度最大的文化遗产。明长城是中国长城的精华，绵延万里横亘于我国北方人口稠密的东北、华北、西北地区，其众多遗存特别是巨大的墙体与公路、铁路、工矿企业、城乡建设以及沿线居民日常生活等产生矛盾难以完全避免。于是，毁坏明长城修路建厂的有之，在城墙上取土、取石用于房屋修葺者有之，在明长城及

其周边开辟耕地、放牧等破坏长城墙体的行为则更是不胜枚举；一些不科学的修复工程和不适当的旅游开发，对明长城及其风貌的破坏也不容小觑；明长城沿线自然环境、气候复杂，地震、山体滑坡、洪水等突发自然灾害时有发生，对长城造成毁灭性破坏的例子并不罕见；风雨侵蚀、环境污染、植物生长、动物破坏等也在悄无声息地威胁着长城的安全。在自然与人为双重因素破坏的共同作用下，明长城保存状况很不乐观，部分地段正逐步丧失其原貌，甚至走向消失。

为了应对日益严重的人为和自然因素破坏威胁，20世纪80年代以来，长城沿线各省、自治区、直辖市的文物部门曾对长城做过不同程度的专题调查，初步掌握了长城保存的基本情况。限于当时的条件和认识水平，对长城相关情况的掌握和资料储备等，尚远不能满足长城保护、管理、研究等的需要。这种状况严重制约了长城保护政策法规的出台和执行，严重影响了具体保护规划、措施的制定和实施，已经成为长城保护、研究等工作深入开展的瓶颈。采取有效措施，彻底改变长城家底不清，进而扭转长城保护工作的被动局面，已经成为文物保护界的共识，同时也是社会各界广为关注的焦点。为彻底扭转长城保护面临的严峻形势，国家文物局果断提出开展长城保护工程和长城资源调查工作。

明长城资源调查是长城资源调查工作的第一阶段，也是全国长城资源调查的开端和重点。该项目除了完成明长城资源田野调查、数据整理、资料整合，测量明长城长度，生产明长城基础地理信息和专题要素数据，发布明长城长度等重要信息，建

立明长城记录档案和明长城资源信息系统等工作任务，全面、准确掌握明长城的规模、分布、构成、走向、自然与人文环境、保护与管理现状等基础资料，达到为编制明长城保护规划、开展明长城保护工程、加强明长城保护管理和科学研究提供科学依据的目的以外，还肩负着为整个长城资源调查摸索经验、培养和锻炼队伍的重任。

明长城资源调查是对中国境内全部明长城遗存进行首次综合性专题科学调查。其调查范围之广、难度之高、数据量之大，可谓前所未有，当然也就不存在现成经验可以照搬。因此，为保证调查的全面性、科学性、系统性和规范性，从根本上杜绝各种可能出现的混乱问题，科学确定调查工作的组织机构和制度、调查方法和步骤以及技术路线等就显得十分重要。

长城资源调查项目由国家文物局统一规划部署。从2004年春开始，国家文物局即针对当时河北、内蒙古、陕西、山东等地连续发生严重破坏长城事件展开调查、处理，并组织部分专业机构和专家起草了长城保护工作方案初稿及相关工作计划。2005年底，经过多次修改完善制订的《"长城保护工程（2005～2014年）"总体工作方案》经国务院领导同志审核同意正式实施。2006年春节前夕，国家文物局在山海关召开长城保护工程启动工作会议，包括长城资源调查工作在内的长城保护工程正式启动。同时，国家文物局成立了由副局长童明康为组长的领导小组，负责《"长城保护工程（2005～2014年）"总体工作方案》有关重大事项的决策和落实工作。领导小组下设由国家文物局相关司室负责人组成的办公室，负责长城保护工程项目实施的组织和协调工作。同时在中国文物研究所（现中国文化遗产研究院）成立长城项目管理组，负责项目实施的具体组织协调、规范管理和成果汇总等工作。

2006年10月，在总结河北、甘肃两省文物、测绘部门合作开展长城资源调查试点工作成功经验的基础上，国家文物局、国家测绘局决定合作开展明长城资源调查。为此，两局联合成立"国家长城资源调查领导小组"，负责长城资源调查的组织、协调及重大问题的决策、统筹安排国家层面的数据整合、建档、建库，以及协调编纂《长城资源调查报告》。国家文物局副局长童明康和国家测绘局副局长李维森任组长，国家文物局文物保护与考古司和国家测绘局国土测绘司共同负责领导小组办公室的工作。2006年12月，两局联合签发文件布置长城资源调查相关工作，标志着文物、测绘两部门合作开展明长城资源调查正式开始。2007年4月，根据国家文物局、国家测绘局的安排，由中国文化遗产研究院牵头，会同国家基础地理信息中心成立"长城资源调查工作项目管理组"（以下简称长城项目组），承担长城资源调查相关具体的日常工作，包括落实领导小组的决策，开展前期调研，起草相关标准规范、各项工作制度，对调查人员进行培训，组织和协调田野调查、内业整理、调查资料汇总、报告编写工作等（图一）。

与此同时，辽宁等明长城沿线10省（自治区、直辖市）文物和测绘部门也根据"国家长城资源调查领导小组"的部署，先后建立了相应的明长城资源调查管理机构，负责组织本省（自治区、直辖市）的明长城资源调查、资料整理、数据整合、建立本省长城记录档案等工作。各省（自治区、直辖市）还任命了本辖区明长城资源调查工作的总领队，根据本省（自治区、直辖市）明长城分布的具体情况组建了调查工作队，具体实施调查工作。据统计，明长城沿线各省（自治区、直辖市）共组建51个调查队，共计有队员448人，其中考古专业人员418人，测绘专业人员30人。

明长城资源调查工作的实施可分为前期准备、全面展开两个阶段。前期准备阶段主要是组建队伍，对调查人员进行全员培训，并开展调查试点，

```
国家文物局  →  领导机制  ←  国家测绘局
                  ↓
                决  策
                  ↓
中国文化遗产研究院   合作机制   国家基础地理信息中心
      ↓                          ↓
    组  织       协调指导        组  织
      ↓                          ↓
长城沿线10个省（自治        长城沿线10个省（自治
区、直辖市）文物部门        区、直辖市）测绘部门
            ↓          ↓
          长城调查、测量
```

图一 明长城资源调查组织示意图

以形成较为成熟的调查队伍和调查方法。同时，通过试点建立一套科学的工作程序，制定并验证一系列技术标准、规范和工作制度，使之具有可操作性和适用性，为长城资源调查工作的全面展开提供经验，避免出现重大失误。

明长城资源调查队主要由考古和测绘专业人员组成。长城资源的复杂性和调查工作的艰巨性，要求调查人员不仅要具有较高的专业素养和丰富的野外工作经验，还要有良好的合作意识，能够正确理解工作任务、意义，进而通过团队的力量来弥补个人能力的不足。为确保调查队伍的综合素质能够满足明长城资源调查工作的需要，除了在组队时对调查队员精挑细选以外，还要对所有参加明长城资源调查的人员进行全员培训。鉴于参加明长城资源调查的人员数量众多，培训工作分为国家、省两级进行。

国家级培训由长城项目组组织实施。培训对象是各省（自治区、直辖市）长城资源调查工作的主要技术负责人和管理人员。培训目标是使学员们通过学习，掌握与本次长城资源调查与测量有关的法律、法规；掌握专门针对本次明长城资源调查与测量制定的技术标准、规范；掌握本次明长城资源调查的工作流程和关键技术环节；为省级培训培养教员等。来自明长城沿线10省（自治区、直辖市）的127名文物、测绘部门的专业技术和管理人员参加了培训。这些学员大都成为各省（自治区、直辖市）明长城资源调查工作的骨干，省级培训也主要由这些人员负责、承担。

省级培训由各省（自治区、直辖市）长城资源调查机构负责，对本辖区参加调查、测量的专业人员进行全员培训。培训目标是经过培训使所有参加长城资源调查的人员熟练掌握所需技术和相关要求，具有独立从事长城资源调查的能力。省级培训同样采取室内授课和野外实习相结合的形式。课程内容与国家级培训大体一致，但针对本地的实际情况有所调整，更具针对性。据统计，省级培训专业人员共计527人。

明长城资源调查采用了田野考古调查与测绘技术手段相结合的方法。针对明长城资源调查工作对象复杂、涉及学科和工作头绪繁多，且参与人员众多的实际情况，为确保本项目科学有序开展，长城项目组先后起草、编制了《长城资源调查工作总体方案》、《全国长城资源调查管理办法》、《长城资源调查资料管理制度》等规章制度。同时，提出了

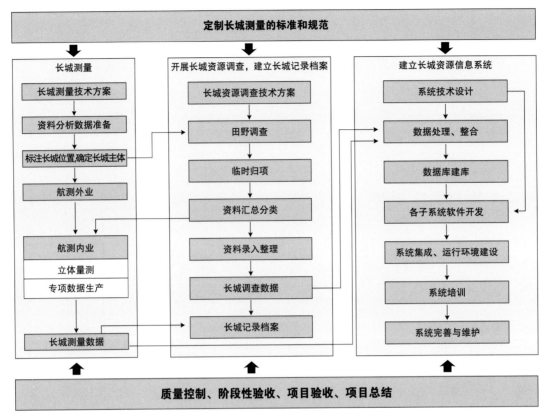

图二 明长城资源调查技术路线图[1]

以"调查与测绘同步、严格数据整合程序"为核心的技术路线（图二）及一系列的技术标准和规范。例如，《长城资源调查工作规程》、《长城资源调查名称使用规范》、《长城资源调查文物编码规则》、《长城资源保存程度评价标准》、《长城基础地理信息与专题要素数据生产外业技术规定》、《长城基础地理信息与专题要素数据生产内业技术规定》、《长城基础地理信息和专题要素数据技术规定》，以及长城墙体调查登记表及著录说明、长城关堡调查登记表及著录说明、长城单体建筑调查登记表及著录说明、长城相关遗存登记表及著录说明、长城调查采（征）集标本登记表、长城GPS采集点登记表和长城资源调查照片登记表、册页等。这些规章制度和标准规范，经国家长城资源调查领导小组审查同意后，大多以不同的方式发布实施，有力地保障了明长城资源调查工作的顺利实施。

田野考古调查是本次明长城资源调查工作的基础和主体，始于2007年4月，2008年11月结束。具体包括前期准备、现场调查确认、数据采集和记录、数据校核和临时归卷、资料数据整理、建立档案（图三）。全国400多名调查队员在两年野外工作中，克服严寒酷暑、荒漠高山等自然环境带来的重重困难，风餐露宿行程数十万公里，徒步对中国境内所有的明长城及相关遗存，进行全覆盖式的实地踏查，对明长城每一段墙体、每一处设施和遗迹都进行详细的调查、记录与测量。调查重点是长城各类遗存本体现状、长城的人文和自然环境、长城保护与管理等方面的情况。具体做法是：调查队首先收集、整理、消化早期文物考古调查、发掘资料，结合历史文献、地方志、民间传说等各类资料相关记载，确定长城的大体走向和布局，并标注在1：50000地形图上，作为工作计划用图，以县级行政区划为单位，划分调查区域。利用1：10000影像图、地形图等作为工作用图，按照事先拟定的工作

[1] 本图引自国家文物局、国家测绘局《长城资源调查工作手册》。

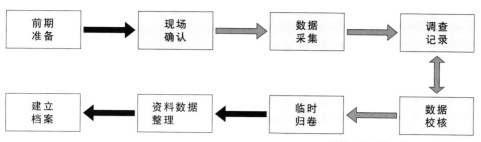

图三　田野调查流程图[2]

计划，对所有明长城遗存进行全面实地调查，采集标本并现场记录、提取数据。在数据采集方面，本次调查充分利用了GPS定位系统、红外测距仪、数码照相机、摄像机等现代设备。填写调查日志和各类登记表格成为调查队员每天必须完成的功课，从而形成了不间断的完整文字记录。

为确保考古田野调查数据质量及方便使用，专门为本次明长城资源调查设计研发了长城田野调查数据采集、检查与汇交系统，用于调查数据的数字化采集与整理。该系统具有三项基本功能：一是田野调查数据管理功能。以县级行政区域为单元，录入和存储长城资源调查文字、多媒体等各类数据，实现县、市（地区）级和省级行政区域的长城资源调查数据汇总，并对其进行查询、管理维护、备份和恢复；二是面向长城田野调查业务的地图应用功能。提供长城资源调查工作需要的地图，辅助应用于调查计划制定、任务安排等；三是长城田野调查数据检查功能。以图像的形式将调查数据与长城基础地理数据进行比对，以检验其准确性。该系统利用GIS（地理信息系统）技术，实现了长城基础地理信息、调查专题信息、调查多媒体等数据的集成管理，做到了实用性与安全性的统一，同时具有可扩充、易维护等特点，为长城资源调查田野数据采集与整理工作提供了有力的支持。

大规模引入数字摄影测量技术等现代科技手段是本次明长城资源调查的一大特色。具体做法是首先根据明

长城的走向与分布，按照国家测绘标准在野外设立控制点，通过对这些点坐标的记录，获取满足长城测量的控制数据（控制点测量与调绘），然后通过立体量测和数据生产等过程，完成室内数据采集，计算并得出明长城的总长度（包括地表长度、投影长度）、分省长度、分类长度（不同建筑材质、保存状况）等数据。同时生产明长城墙体两侧各1千米范围内的基础地理数据（数字线划图（DLG）、数字高程模型（DEM）和数字正射影像图（DOM））、长城专题要素数据（长城本体、附属设施、相关遗存的数字线划图（DLG））。具体流程如图四。

2008年底，明长城资源调查工作进入数据整理阶段。此次调查获得的数据包括长城考古调查各类记录（登记表）22712份、图纸8051张、照片101044张、录像18479段、拓片及摹本66张，数据总量达1043GB；测绘数据有测绘图1970幅（1:10000），DLG、DEM、DOM图2585幅，1:10000分幅长城专题影像图2544幅，分省长城专题影像图10幅，全国明长城分布图1幅，数据量超过200GB。数据整理首先是对长城资源田野调查

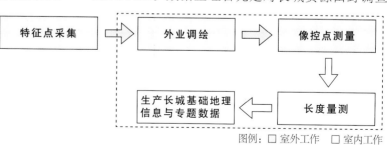

图四　测绘流程图

［2］本图引自国家文物局、国家测绘局《长城资源调查工作手册》。

数据、基础地理数据和相关资料进行整合处理。例如，图文属性连接关系处理；长城本体、附属设施及相关遗存等调查对象的定位处理；生成带状数据拼接处理与编码唯一性处理等。进而形成入库数据：长城资源田野调查数据（长城本体、附属设施及相关遗存等数据），基础地理数据（1:50000基础地理数据、1:10000基础地理数据、1米分辨率影像数据等），相关的文字、图片、多媒体等资料数据等。

有效利用明长城资源数据和基础地理数据为长城保护工程服务是本次明长城资源调查的一个重要目的，为此，研究开发了明长城资源信息系统。该系统以明长城数据库为基础，以基础地理信息为纽带，以标准、制度和安全体系为保障，以长城资源信息管理、利用和研究业务流程为主线，以支撑长城保护为核心，形成数据更新和互联互通、长城资源变化检测、辅助决策支持和社会服务信息化体系。明长城资源信息系统主要包括三个子系统：一是明长城资源信息管理子系统。用于长城资源信息和基础地理信息集成管理、日常维护，实现长城资源调查数据自动装载入库，构建长城资源数据与地理数据关联等；二是明长城资源信息应用子系统。主要面向长城保护、利用、管理和研究的应用需要，逐步实现长城资源数据统计查询、长城数字记录档案查看、长城专题图制作等，并根据长城保护工程需要，逐步发展其他方面的应用功能；三是明长城资源信息公众服务子系统。利用WebGIS（网络地理信息系统）技术，将长城资源信息和长城保护有关法律法规发布于互联网上，使社会公众足不出户就能查询和浏览明长城基本信息，同时也可就长城保护发表自己的意见和建议。此外，在文物系统没有政府专网链接的情况下，该子系统可为省级文物部门设立专门通道，服务于长城资源数据更新工作，从而保持长城资源数据的现势性。

二、成果丰硕，意义深远

明长城是由墙体、敌台、马面、烽火台、关隘、城堡等多种设施组成的，功能完备，具有广阔战略纵深的军事防御体系。同时，它也是中原农耕文明与草原游牧文明交流、融合的通道与纽带，具有极高的文物价值与研究价值。本次明长城资源调查全面、准确地掌握了明长城的历史沿革、规模、分布、构成、走向，自然与人文环境，保护与管理现状等方面的情况，收获颇丰。

通过本次调查，可以确认明长城修筑于14世纪至16世纪，东起辽宁省丹东市的虎山，西至甘肃省嘉峪关，大体呈东西走向，行经辽宁、河北、天津、北京、山西、内蒙古、陕西、宁夏、甘肃、青海10个省（自治区、直辖市），由墙体、敌台、马面、烽火台、关堡、壕沟、挡马墙、品字窖、火池、烟灶、驿站等设施组成。同时，长城沿线还有大量与长城建设和使用有关的碑碣、题刻、戍卒墓地、砖瓦窑、采石场、居住址、水窖、寺庙、马市等遗存。

明长城墙体可分为人工墙体、壕堑、自然险三大类。其中，人工墙体可根据建造材质的不同，分为土墙、石墙、砖墙、山险墙（利用自然山体、沟壑等，通过人工铲削、砌石或夯土修整形成）等类别；自然险可分为山险、河险两类；壕堑是指在平地上人工挖掘土壕形成防御屏障。经量测，明长城的坡面总长度为8851.79千米（测量精度为±312.95米），投影长度8629.36千米（参见《明长城》（分省）调查长度统计表），约一万七千余华里，可见文献所载"万里长城"不虚。其中，人工墙体总长6259.6千米，占明长城总长度的70.8%；壕堑总长359.7千米，占明长城总长度的4%；天然险总长

明长城（分省）调查长度统计表

	任务分区 （省、自治区、直辖市）	坡面长度 （千米）	投影长度 （千米）
1	北京	526.65	489.31
2	天津	40.28	36.93
3	河北	1338.63	1283.66
4	山西	896.53	868.35
5	内蒙古	712.57	706.42
6	辽宁	1218.81	1198.53
7	陕西	1218.06	1199.38
8	甘肃	1699.25	1689.06
9	青海	363.44	341.35
10	宁夏	837.58	816.36
	合 计	8851.79	8629.36

2232.5千米，占明长城总长度的25.2%。明长城人工墙体保存状况不一。依据《长城资源保存程度评价标准》，保存较好的513.5千米，保存一般的1104.4千米，保存较差的1494.7千米，保存差的1185.4千米，地面无存的1961.6千米。

在长城墙体及其沿线附近，建有敌台、马面、烽火台等结构、功能各异的单体建筑以及关堡等设施。具体数据为：敌台7062座、马面3357座、烽火台5723座、关堡1176处、壕沟、挡马墙、品字窖（也称陷马坑）、火池、烟灶、驿站（递铺、驿馆、驿递）等设施467处，碑碣、题刻、刻石、戍卒墓地、砖瓦窑、采石场、居住址、水窖、寺庙、马市等与明长城相关的遗存559处，共计16142处。

明长城绵延万里，不同地区的遗存具有鲜明的地域性特点。辽宁、河北、天津、 北京的墙体及相关设施以砖石建造者较为常见，应与这里靠近京师，是防御重点且盛产石材有关；山西、陕西、宁夏、内蒙古、甘肃、青海的长城墙体和相关设施则以黄土夯筑者最为常见。

除了有史以来第一次准确量测并得到明长城长度、各类设施准确数量等基本数据以外，本次明长城资源调查还新发现了一批长城遗迹。据初步统计，各地新发现的长城遗迹有400余处。由于资料整理、研究工作尚未完成，在此仅列举一二。北京市大庄科、海字口等处新发现5千米墙体、与明长城相关的1处冶铁遗址和多处窑址以及采石场遗址等；甘肃省新发现明长城墙体及壕堑3段、关堡6座、单体建筑4座。发现了烽火台筑在壕堑中央的特殊做法。基本搞清了一直以来被认为线路比较复杂的古浪县明长城走向和一直以来不甚清楚的兰州市辖区和白银市部分县区的明长城走向问题等；河北省迁安市发现镶在城墙上的"东协燕河路西界"、"中协太平路东界"界碑两块，搞清了明代蓟镇所辖太平路与燕河路的分界。发现在隘口或地势偏低平坦的地方，毛石墙顶多处设有规律、形状多为椭圆形、大小仅容一人、成组的单兵防御掩体。赤城县龙关镇发现保存完好的片石墙体373米。沽源县境内发现一条通往"开平卫"的烽燧线等；辽宁省新发现二台子路河、康家路河、连城路河、龙山路河、七台子路河、三台子路河、四台子路河、万家壕路河、五台子路河等河险墙。锦州市黑山县白厂门镇石家沟村翟家屯发现8条长约800米平行且保存较好的长城墙体，颇为壮观。位于凌海市温滴楼乡大茂堡村的大茂堡城仍保存较好，其圆角城台等建筑，在已发现的堡城中较为罕见；内蒙古自治区鄂尔多斯市新发现的长城，修正了以往学术界关于明宁夏镇两道边西端交汇点具体位置的认识，即该交汇点在清水营堡北面，而非兴武营堡北面，两者相差甚远；宁夏回族自治区海原县境内发现一处长17358米长城墙体，为历次调查中所未见；青海省湟中县发现了丰台沟壕堑和坡西壕堑，乐都县发现石家沟壕堑，湟中县上新庄题刻墨书20个字，记述了修筑长城用工；山西省繁峙县境内发现茨沟营南岭长城、西岭长城、白头沟长城均为石墙。左权县黄泽关堡内发现的"新修十八盘并天井郊城堡图"石碑，详细描绘了黄泽关堡、关门和关道的位置、格局；陕西省定边县发现被沙漠掩埋的烽火台、马面及墙体，榆阳区新发现76千米长城、33座烽火台、74座敌台、97座马面、24处堡等遗存。

清代以降，长城因失去了其原有功能而日渐荒芜、废弃，并因自然灾害、战乱及人们生产生活等因素的破坏而逐渐残破，部分段落甚至彻底消失。新中国成立以后，长城保护管理和研究工作逐步改善。20世纪50年代起，各级政府、文物部门陆续开展了一些对明长城的调查工作。山海关、八达岭、荆紫关、嘉峪关等部分长城段落被国务院以及各级地方政府分期分批公布为全国重点文物保护单位、省级及市县级文物保护单位；相关地方政府为辖区内的部分长城划定了保护范围和建设控制地带，有的设立了专门的保护管理机构。期间，对八达岭、慕田峪、居庸关等重要长城段落进行了不同规模、程度的保护修缮；1987年，长城整体列入《世界遗产名录》；与此同时，各级政府逐步依法加大对破坏长城案件的查处力度。但从整体上讲，明长城的保护和管理工作远未达到理想状态，这也是将保护管理状况列入本次明长城资源调查的重要原因。

明长城作为一个文物保护单位[3]，其直接的保护管理工作由一个专门机构承担最为理想。由于历史、体制等方面的原因，明长城一直采取属地管理的方式进行保护管理，由所在地市县文化文物部门负责。据此次调查初步统计，全国参与明长城管理的各类机构有183个。具体管理方式多种多样：由政府文物主管部门委托当地文物保护管理所或者博物馆等专业机构兼管，没有专门的长城保护管理机构，这种方式占大部分；部分地方政府文物部门采取聘请长城保护员对属地长城及相关设施进行看

护，也有和当地乡镇签订长城保护责任书。如河北、北京、宁夏部分市县；由政府设置的专门保护管理机构负责。这些专门机构一般设于重要或知名的长城关隘或段落等地方。如河北省的山海关、金山岭，天津市的黄崖关，北京市的居庸关、八达岭，陕西省的镇北台、红石峡、榆林卫城和易马城等。这些专门机构的隶属多种多样，有政府派出机构（北京市居庸关）、旅游部门（天津市蓟县八仙山风景区管理局）；个别地方由社会团体对长城实施简单的看护管理，如陕西省神木县长城保护协会。明长城分布在10个省级行政区域，部分长城是省市县甚至乡镇之间的分界线，不同行政区域交界处的长城如何管理、责权利如何划分也是长城保护管理中需要注意的问题。

划定保护范围和建设控制地带是对文物保护单位保护管理方面的基本要求。本次调查表明，明长城保护范围和建设控制地带划定工作在各地的进展参差不齐。辽宁省对已公布为省级及以上文物保护单位的明长城段落，划定了相应的保护范围和建设控制地带；北京市文物局、北京市规划委员会根据《北京市长城保护管理办法》、《北京市文物保护单位保护范围及建设控制地带管理规定》等法规，为北京市境内的明长城划定了临时保护范围和建设控制地带（长城墙体两侧500米；长城墙体两侧500米至3000米）；河北省人民政府发布《河北省人民政府关于印发〈河北省国家级、省级文物保护单位保护范围及建设控制地带〉的通知》，划定了境内26个县的明长城保护范围和建设控制地带。其中墙体以墙基外缘为基线，向两侧各外扩50米为保护范围，以保护范围边线为基础，向两侧各外扩100米为建设控制地带。单体设施（烽火台、敌台、战

---

[3] 从第六批全国重点文物保护单位开始，国务院将"长城"作为一个单位公布。

台、关隘等）以基础外缘为基线，四周各外扩50米为保护范围，以基础外缘为基线，四周各外扩100米为建设控制地带。宣府镇城以城墙基础两侧外皮为基线，内外两侧各扩展30米为保护范围，以保护范围边线为基线，内外两侧各扩展70米为建设控制地带；山西省黄泽关堡、关门，盘垴村东南侧长城和白皮关关门，口上村东侧长城1段、口上村东侧敌台6处明长城遗迹划定了保护范围和建设控制地带；陕西省横山县、靖边县、吴起县及榆林市榆阳区等地共有10处明长城设立了保护范围；宁夏回族自治区中卫县、灵武市政府将境内长城两侧各50米划定为保护范围，两侧各100米为建设控制地带；青海省仅有被公布为省级文物保护单位的大通县桥头镇明长城划定了长城本体两侧各50米为保护范围和建设控制地带；甘肃省永昌县将境内长城墙体两侧各10米范围划为保护范围和建设控制地带，永登县将明长城及烽火台遗迹四周外20米设为保护范围，保护范围向外顺延150米为建设控制地带，嘉峪关市早在1968年就划定了嘉峪关关城保护范围及其四至，山丹县规定长城墙体两侧各15米为保护范围、40米为建设控制地带。天津市和内蒙古自治区境内的明长城尚未划定保护范围和建设控制地带。

设置保护标志和建立科学的记录档案是文物保护单位的法定保护措施之一。据本次调查，已列为各级文物保护单位的明长城大都设置了保护标志，计237处。未列为文物保护单位的长城，绝大部分没有设立规范的保护标志。与此类似，除已公布为全国重点文物保护单位的长城点段建立了记录档案外，其他部分明长城档案几近空白。本次明长城资源调查工作的一项重要任务就是全面建立明长城记录档案，相信其一定会为长城保护维修、展示与利用等提供有力的资料支持。

The Results of the Investigation and Measurement of the Ming Great Wall Resources

Chai Xiaoming and Yang Zhaojun

How long at all is the Great Wall? It seems to be an easy question because every Chinese even many people in the world know that China has a "Ten-thousand li Great Wall". However, it is also a hard issue of many professional people in the academic fields: since the first Great Wall emerged in China, no one has known the exact answer. In the recent years, the natural weathering and artificial damaging are making the scholars and the public society worry more and more about the Great Wall. In the early 2005, the State Administration of Cultural Heritage (SACH hereafter) edited *The General Plan of the Great Wall Protection Project (2005-2014)* and was approved by the State Council. This plan defined that the short-term objectives of the Great Wall Protection Project are to make clear the details of the properties of the Great Wall, to establish and perfect the relevant laws, rules and regulations and to straighten out the management mechanism, in order to arrange the scientific maintenance and rational utilization of the Great Wall, strengthen the supervision and management, thoroughly prevent the damaging of the Great Wall and lay a firm foundation for the positive development of the preservation of the Great Wall under a unified direction and plan. First of all, to make clear the details of the "properties" -- the Great Wall resources investigation is the primary task which is listed as the first item in the Great Wall Protection Project. The Ming Great Wall resources investigation is the first stage of the entire Great Wall resources investigation Project; to date, this project has mostly finished with rich achievements.

1. The Unified Planning and the Innovative Cooperation

The Great Wall has giant size and system, rich remains and is located in diversified and complicated natural environments, all of which make it the cultural heritage most difficult to protect. Ming Great Wall, which is the essence of the Great Walls of all of the periods, spreads in the densely populated Northeast, North and Northwest China, because of which its numerous and various remains, especially the massive wall body, will unavoidably have conflicts with the traffic lines, industrial enterprises, urban and rural constructions and the daily lives of the residents along its courses. In fact, the cases of demolishing the Great Wall to clear space for building roads or factories, fetching earth, brick and stone from the Great

Wall to build or amend houses, opening farmlands or pasture nearby the Great Wall which are eroding and nibbling the wall bodies are occurring here and there frequently. Some improper amending projects and unsuitable tourism developments are also damaging the Ming Great Wall and the surrounding landscapes. The geographic, geological and climatic conditions in the areas through which the Great Wall goes are very complicated; earthquakes, landslides and floods and other natural disasters are usually tend to take place and damage and even destroy some parts of the Great Wall. The weathering, environment pollution, plant growing and animal tunneling are also threatening the Great Wall. Under the double effects from natural and artificial powers, the preservation status of the Ming Great Wall is not optimistic: some sections are losing their original features and some sections are even disappearing.

To deal with the threats of the daily-increasing artificial and natural damaging, since the early 1980s, subject investigations of various levels have been conducted in many regions by which the outlined preservation status of the Great Wall was preliminarily understood. However, limited by the then conditions and knowledge level, the information and data reservation on the Great Wall were far from meeting the demand of the preservation, management and researches on the Great Wall. This situation severely restricted the setting forth and execution of the policies and regulations on the Great Wall protection and the designing and practicing of the concrete protection plans and measures, so it has become the bottleneck of the in-depth development of the preservation and research works on the Great Wall. To apply effective measures to make clear the property of the Great Wall and change the unfavorable status has become the consensus of the cultural heritage protection discipline, and also the focus to which the attention of the people of all walks of lives paid. To change the severe situation of the Great Wall protection, SACH decided to conduct the Great Wall Protection Project and the Great Wall resources investigation.

The Ming Great Wall resources investigation is the first step and the incipient and key step of the investigation of the Great Wall resources. In addition to its own duties, which are the fulfillments of the field investigation, data processing, material integration, the length measuring of the Ming Great Wall, the basic geographic information and thematic data producing, record archive building, Ming Great Wall Resource Information System building to comprehensively and accurately grasp the scale, distribution, composition, courses and natural and humanistic environments of the Ming Great Wall in order to provide scientific evidences for the designing of the Ming Great Wall Protection Project and strengthening the management and researches on the Ming Great Wall, this investigation project also has the duty of accumulating experiences and organizing and training personnel for the entire Great Wall resources investigation being conducted in the future.

The Ming Great Wall resources investigation is the first scientific comprehensive subject investigation to the Great Wall built in the Ming Dynasty, the range of investigation, the difficulty and the data amount of which are all unprecedented and certainly no well done experiences could be referred to. Therefore, to guarantee the investigation to be comprehensive, scientific, systematic and normative, to thoroughly prevent all possible mistakes and confusions from happen at the very beginning, to scientifically arrange the organization and rules of the investigation and to define the investigation methods, procedure and technical lines are all very important.

The Great Wall resources investigation project is planned and arranged by the SACH. Since the spring of 2004, the SACH directed the investigations and handlings of the cases of the severe damaging of the Great Wall in Hebei, Inner Mongolia, Shaanxi and Shandong Provinces and organized some institutions and experts to draft the plans of the Great Wall Protection Project and the related jobs. At the end of 2005, *the General Plan for the Great Wall Protection Project (2005-2014)* was approved by the leaders of the State Council after revised and perfected for many times and put into effect. On the eve of the Spring Festival of 2006, the SACH held the meeting for the starting of the Great Wall Protection Project in Shanhaiguan, by which the Great Wall Protection Project including the Great Wall resource investigation was started. At the same time, the SACH established the Great Wall Protection Project Leading Group headed by Deputy Director Tong Mingkang in charge of the decision and enforcement of the important affairs of *The General Plan for the Great Wall Protection Project (2005-2014)*. Under the leading group, the office consisting of the leaders of the relevant departments and bureaus is in charge of the organizing

and coordinating of the enforcement of the project. In Chinese Academy of Cultural Heritage, a Great Wall Project Managing Group is established in charge of organizing, coordinating, regulating and managing the concrete jobs and reviewing and compiling the results of the protection projects.

In October 2006, with the reference of the experiences of the trial cooperative investigation of the Great Wall resources conducted by the cultural heritage and surveying institutions of Hebei and Gansu Provinces, the SACH and the National Administration of Surveying, Mapping and Geoinformation (then State Bureau of Surveying and Mapping, SBSM hereafter) decided to jointly conduct the Ming Great Wall resources investigation, for which the "State Great Wall Resources Investigation Leading Group" consisting of officials of these two administrations was established. This group is jointly headed by Mr. Tong Mingkang, the deputy director of the SACH and Mr. Li Weisen, the deputy director of SBSM, and the Cultural Relics Protection and Archaeology Department of SACH and the Department of National Land Survey of SBSM are jointly in charge of the office affairs. In December 2006, the two administrations jointly issued documents to arrange the Great Wall resources investigation, which symbolizes the formal starting of the cooperation of the Ming Great Wall resources investigation. In April 2007, according to the arrangement of SACH and SBSM, the Chinese Academy of Cultural Heritage and National Geomatics Center of China (NGCC hereafter) organized the "Great Wall Resources Investigation Project Managing Group" to carry out the routine affairs, including the enforcement of the decisions of the State Great Wall Resources Investigation Leading Group, the preparative investigations and studies, the drafting of the relevant standards, regulations and working procedures, the training of the personnel, the organization and coordination of the fieldwork, the office work, the collecting of the investigation materials and the composing of the reports (Figure 1).

Meanwhile, the cultural heritage and surveying administrations and institutions of the ten provinces (or autonomous regions and municipalities) through which the Great Wall goes also established their local management and execution agencies according to the plan of the State Great Wall Resources Investigation Leading Group to direct and manage

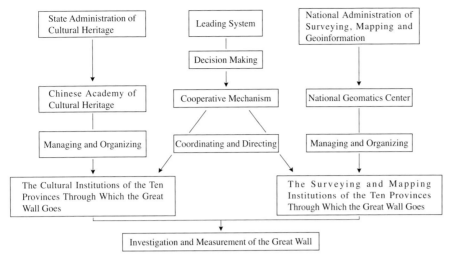

Figure 1   The Organization of the Investigation of the Ming Great Wall Resources

the investigation, material collection, data integration and record archive building of the sections of the Great Wall within their respective administrative areas. Each administrative area has assigned the general leader of the Great Wall resources investigation and organized the investigation team to conduct the investigation job. As the statistics, 51 investigation teams are organized in the ten provinces (or autonomous regions and municipalities), including 448 team members, 418 among whom are archaeologists and 30 are surveyors.

The conduction of the Ming Great Wall resources investigation consisted of the beforehand preparation step and complete launching step. The tasks of the first step was mainly organizing teams, training personnel, conducting trial investigations to get mature investigation teams and suitable methods. Meanwhile, through the trial investigations, a scientific working procedure was established, a series of technical standards, regulations and working rules were designed and verified to be operable and serviceable and experiences are provided to the comprehensive development of the Great Wall resources investigation so that severe errors and mistakes can be avoided.

The investigation teams consisted mainly of the professional archaeologists and surveyors. The complexity of the Great Wall resources and the difficulty of the investigation fieldwork required the investigators not only the professional qualifications and fieldwork experiences but also good teamwork awareness, as well as correct and accurate understandings to the objectives and significances of their task, by which they could make up their insufficient personal abilities by the strength of the teamwork. To guarantee the qualifications of the investigation teams to meet the jobs' demand, except for the careful selection of the team members, overall trainings were done to all of the members selected for this task. Because of the large number of the investigators being trained, the trainings were conducted in national and provincial levels.

The national training was conducted by the Great Wall Resources Investigation Project Managing Group, the trainees of which were the technical leaders and managers of the teams, and the goals were making them grasp the laws and rules related to the Great Wall resource investigation and measurement, the technical standards and regulations designed specially for this

investigation, the workflows and the key technical links of the field and office work and training instructors for the provincial training programs. 127 technical and management leaders from the ten provinces (autonomous regions and municipalities) through which the Great Wall goes attended the training, most of whom became the core members of the investigation teams and the trainers of the team members of the related provinces.

The provincial training programs were run by the Great Wall investigation administrations and institutions of the relevant provincial level administrative areas, the tasks of which were the all-member training to the investigation teams of the Great Wall resources. The objectives of the trainings were making all of the investigators thoroughly grasp the needed techniques and requirements and have the ability of independently conducting the Great Wall resources investigation. The provincial training programs also applied both the indoor instructing and field practicing methods, the contents of which were roughly the same as that of the national training programs, but slightly modified to match the local conditions. In total 527 team members attended the provincial training programs.

The Ming Great Wall resources investigation integrated the archaeological field surveying and geographic surveying. In the light of the complicated investigation objects, the diversified disciplines and issues involved and the numerous participants, to guarantee this project to be conducted orderly and scientifically, the Great Wall Resources Investigation Project Managing Group drafted and compiled *The General Plan of the Great Wall Protection Project (2005-2014), The Management Procedure of the National Great Wall Resource Investigation* and other regulations. Meanwhile, the Managing Group set forth the technical procedure (Figure 2) centered by the principle of "synchronize the investigation and measurement and strictly execute the data collecting rules" and a series of technical standards and regulations. For example, *The Operation Rules of the Great Wall Resources Investigation, The Nomenclature of the Great Wall Resources Investigation, The Coding Rules of the Great Wall Resources Investigation, The Standard of the Preservation Status Evaluation of the Great Wall Resources, The Technical Regulations of the Basic Geographic Information and Subject Data Producing Fieldwork, The Technical Regulations of the Basic Geographic Information and Subject Data Producing Office Work,* The Great Wall Body Registration Form, the Great Wall Fortress and Garrison Registration Form, the Great Wall Independent Architecture Registration Form, the Great Wall Relevant Remains Registration Form and their respective registration instructions, and the Gathered (Acquired) Artifact Registration Form, the Great Wall GPS Feature Point Registration Form, the Great Wall Resource Investigation Photograph Registration Form and Album, and so on. These regulations and standards are issued and enforced

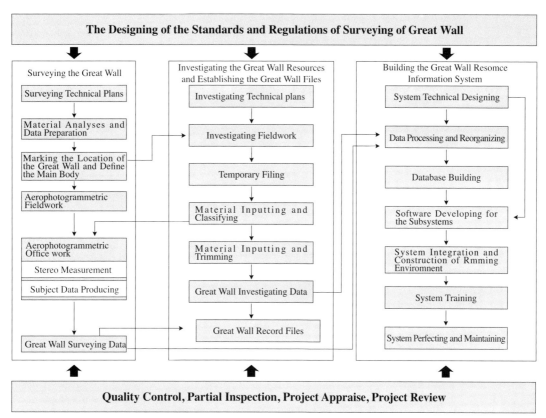

The Designing of the Standards and Regulations of Surveying of Great Wall

Surveying the Great Wall
- Surveying Technical Plans
- Material Analyses and Data Preparation
- Marking the Location of the Great Wall and Define the Main Body
- Aerophotogrammetric Fieldwork
- Aerophotogrammetric Office work
- Stereo Measurement
- Subject Data Producing
- Great Wall Surveying Data

Investigating the Great Wall Resources and Establishing the Great Wall Files
- Investigating Technical plans
- Investigating Fieldwork
- Temporary Filing
- Material Inputting and Classifying
- Material Inputting and Trimming
- Great Wall Investigating Data
- Great Wall Record Files

Building the Great Wall Resomce Information System
- System Technical Designing
- Data Processing and Reorganizing
- Database Building
- Software Developing for the Subsystems
- System Integration and Construction of Rmming Environment
- System Training
- System Perfecting and Maintaining

Quality Control, Partial Inspection, Project Appraise, Project Review

Figure 2　The Technical Procedure of the Investigation and Measurement of the Ming Great Wall Resources[1]

after being reviewed and approved by the State Great Wall Resources Investigation Leading Group and powerfully assured the conduction of the Ming Great Wall resources investigation Project.

The archaeological field surveying, which is the foundation and main task of this Ming Great Wall resources investigation, was started in April 2007 and completed in November 2008. The whole procedure included the beforehand preparation, onsite confirmation, data gathering and investigation recording, data checking and calibrating, temporary filing, data trimming and archives building (Figure 3). In the two years of fieldwork, the over 400 investigators walked hundreds of thousands of kilometers on foot in the mountains, deserts, grasslands and various weathers, made a full-coverage onsite investigation to the whole Ming Great Wall and related remains in China, and carefully surveyed, recorded and measured every section of wall body, every facility and every piece of the remains. The foci of this investigation are the status quo of all of the remains of and related to the Great Wall, the humanistic and natural environments, the statuses of the preservation and management of the Great Wall, and so on. At first, the investigators collected, reviewed and digested the materials of the past archaeological reconnaissances and excavations, referred to the historic literature, local chronicles, folk legends and other textural materials, outlined the rough orientations and distributions of the Ming Great Wall and marked them on the topographic maps to the scale of 1:50000 as the working plan maps and zoned the investigation areas by the county-level administrative areas.

They used the image maps and topographic maps to the scale of 1:10000 as the working reference maps to conduct the overall onsite investigations to all of the remains of and related to the Ming Great Wall, gather the artifacts, samples and draw data. For the data gathering, the GPS, infrared EDM instrument, digital camera, digital video camera and other modern equipments were used. Writing investigation log and filling out the registration forms are the daily homework of the investigation teammates, by which the uninterrupted textural records are preserved.

To keep the quality of the archaeological fieldwork in an easy way, a data gathering, checking and uploading system is developed for this Great Wall resources investigation to acquire, store and process the digitized data. This system has three basic functions: the first is the fieldwork data managing function. The textual and multimedia data of the Great Wall resources investigation are input and stored into this system by county level administrative area as the top storage unit, and the data of the county, city (region) and province levels can be collected, inquired, managed, maintained, backed up and restored. The second is the fieldwork-oriented map supplying function. The system provides all of the maps for the fieldwork of the Great Wall resources investigation to assist the drafting of the investigation plans and arranging the tasks. The third is the data calibrating function. This system compares the data extracted in the investigation with the basic geographic information data of the Great Wall in the image format to check their accuracy. With the GIS technology, this system fulfilled the integrated managements of the basic geographic information data,

---

[1]. This figure is quoted from The Great Wall Resources Investigation Manual edited and issued by the SACH and SBSM.

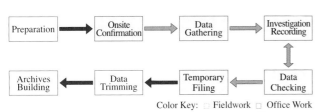

Color Key: ☐ Fieldwork ☐ Office Work

Figure 3　The Workflow of the Investigation Fieldwork[1]

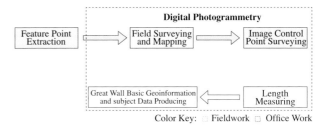

Color Key: ☐ Fieldwork ☐ Office Work

Figure 4　The Workflow of the Measurement of the Ming Great Wall

thematic data of the Great Wall resources investigation and the multimedia data collected in the investigation and accomplished the practicality and safety as well as the scalability and easy maintenance. This system provided powerful support to the fieldwork data acquiring and storing of the Great Wall resources investigation.

The Large-scale application of modern scientific and technological methods such as digital photogrammetry is one of the characteristics of this Ming Great Wall resources investigation. The concrete procedure is: first, the feature points are selected in the field according to the national measuring standards and based on the course and distribution of the Ming Great Wall to fetch the control data (the field surveying and mapping of the feature points), then the indoor data gathering is done through stereo measurement and data production by calculating the full length (including the ground length and projected length), provincial lengths and classified lengths (by building materials, preservation status, etc.) and other data. Meanwhile, the basic geographic data of the zone 1 km wide from the both sides of the Ming Great Wall (including the digital line graphics [DLG], digital elevation models [DEM] and digital orthophoto maps [DOM]) and the thematic data of the Great Wall (the digital line graphics of the wall bodies, auxiliary facilities and relevant remains) are also produced. The concrete workflow is seen as Figure 4.

At the end of 2008, the project of the Ming Great Wall resources investigation entered the stage of data processing. The investigation accumulated 22712 records (charts and registration forms) of all subjects, 8051 drawings, 101044 photographs, 18479 video clips, 66 rubbings and replicas, the total data volume of which is as huge as 1043 gigabytes; the measurement acquired 1970 maps (1:10000 scale), 2585 DLG, DEM and DOM, 2544 subdivided thematic image maps of the Great Wall (1:10000 scale), 10 provincial thematic image maps of the Great Wall and one general distribution map of the Ming Great Wall, the total data volume of which is as huge as over 200 gigabytes. The first step of the data producing is the integration of the field investigation data, basic geographic data and other data relevant to the Great Wall resources. For example, the image-text attribution association, the positioning of the investigation objects, such as the main body of the Great Wall, the auxiliary facilities and relevant remains, the striped data bridging and unique coding processing, and so on, by which the data being warehoused are produced: the Great Wall resources field

investigation data (data of the main body, the auxiliary facilities and relevant remains of the Great Wall), basic geographic data (1:50000 basic geographic data, 1:10000 basic geographic data, 1 m resolution image data, etc.), the relevant textual, pictorial and multimedia data, and so on.

Effectively utilizing the Ming Great Wall resource data and basic geographic data to serve the Great Wall Protection Project is one of the important objectives of this Ming Great Wall resources investigation. In order to fulfill this objective, we developed the Ming Great Wall Resources Information System. This information system formed the data updating and transferring, resource alteration monitoring and examining and social service information systems with the Ming Great Wall resource database as the backbone, the basic geographic information as the approach, the standards, regulations and security system as the guarantees, the academic workflow of the Great Wall resource information management, utilization and research as the main line and supporting the Great Wall protection as the central task. The Ming Great Wall Resources Information System mainly consists of three subsystems: the first is the Ming Great Wall Resource Information Management Subsystem, which is for the integrative management and routine maintenance of the Great Wall resources information and basic geographic information, the fulfillment of the automatic loading of the Great Wall resources investigation data and the establishment of the association of the Great Wall resources investigation data and the geographic data; the second is the Ming Great Wall Resources Application Subsystem, which is for meeting the demands of the protection, utilization, management and researches of the Great Wall by gradually fulfilling the Great Wall resource data statistics and inquiry service, the search and review service of the Great Wall digital archives and the making of the subject images of the Great Wall, and developing other applicative functions; the third is the Ming Great Wall Resource Information Public Service Subsystem, which publishes the Ming Great Wall resource information and related rules and regulations on the Internet with WebGIS technology so that the people can search and browse the general information of the Ming Great Wall and publish their opinions and suggestions on the Great Wall protection without leaving home. Moreover, in the situation that the cultural heritage administrations don't have the dedicated government web service, this subsystem can provide special line for the provincial cultural heritage administrations to upload and update the Great Wall resource data and to keep their

[1]. This figure is quoted from The Great Wall Resources Investigation Manual edited and issued by the SACH and SBSM.

No.	Mission Area	Ground Length (km)	Projected Length (km)
1	Beijing	526.65	489.31
2	Tianjin	40.28	36.93
3	Hebei	1338.63	1283.66
4	Shanxi	896.53	868.35
5	Inner Mongolia	712.57	706.42
6	Liaoning	1218.81	1198.53
7	Shaanxi	1218.06	1199.38
8	Gansu	1699.25	1689.06
9	Qinghai	363.44	341.35
10	Ningxia	837.58	816.36
	Sum	8851.79	8629.36

currency.

2. The Abundant Achievements and the Profound Significances

The Ming Great Wall consisting of the walls, watchtowers, pass fortresses, guard garrisons, beacon towers and other facilities was a military defense system with complete functions and strategic depth. Meanwhile, it was also the passage and link for the agricultural civilizations in the Central Plains and the nomadic civilizations in the northern steppes to communicate and interact; therefore, it has high cultural and academic values. This Ming Great Wall resources investigation comprehensively and accurately grasped the evolution, scale, distribution, composition, courses and orientations, the natural and humanistic environments and the preservation and management statuses of the Ming Great Wall and got rich results.

This investigation confirmed that the Ming Great Wall was built in the 14th through 16th centuries, starting from the Hushan Hill in Dandong City, Liaoning Province and ending at Jiayuguan Pass in Gansu Province; roughly running in east-west orientation through Liaoning, Hebei, Tianjin, Beijing, Shanxi, Inner Mongolia, Shaanxi, Ningxia, Gansu and Qinghai, totally ten provinces (autonomous regions and municipalities); it consisted of the wall bodies, watchtowers, bastions, beacon towers, passes and fortresses, trenches, stockades, triangle horse pitfalls, fire nests, smoke hearths, post stations and other defense facilities. Meanwhile, along the courses of the Ming Great Wall, there are also large amounts of remains related to the construction and use of the Great Wall, such as the tablets and inscriptions, warrior cemeteries, brick kilns, quarries, residential areas, water cisterns, temples and horse markets, and so on.

The bodies of the Ming Great Wall could be classified into artificial walls, trenches and natural barriers. Of them, the artificial walls again could be classified by the materials into earthen walls, stone walls, brick walls and steep mountain walls (formed by steepening the natural cliffs, slopes or canyons, and filling the gaps by laying bricks or stones or ramming earth). The natural barriers could again be classified into mountain barriers and river barriers. Trenches are the defensive ditches dug in the plain areas in stead of walls or as the auxiliary facilities of the walls. The measuring result is that the general ground length of the Ming Great Wall is 8851.79 km (± 312.95 m) and the projected length is 8629.36 km (See Table), or more than 17000 li, which proved that the "Ten-thousand li Great Wall" is not just a metaphor. Of this length, the artificial walls took 6259.6 km, which is 70.8% of the general length; trenches took 359.7 km, which is 4% of the general length; natural barriers took 2232.5 km, which is 25.2% of the general length. The preservation statuses of the artificial wall bodies vary sharply: according to the Standard of the Preservation Status Evaluation of the Great Wall Resources, 513.5 km of the artificial walls are in good condition, 1104.4 km are in mean condition, 1494.7 km are in poor condition, 1185.4 km are in bad condition and 1961.6 km are completely demolished without ground structure remaining.

Nearby the wall bodies of the Great Wall or along their courses, the independent or attached architectures and facilities of various functions were built, including watchtowers, bastions, beacon towers, fortresses, and so on. Their exact data are as the following: 7062 watchtowers, 3357 bastions, 5723 beacon towers, 1176 fortresses and garrisons, 467 trenches, stockades, triangle horse pitfalls, fire nests, smoke hearths, post stations and other defense facilities, 559 tablets and inscriptions, warrior cemeteries, brick kilns, quarries, residential areas, water cisterns, temples and horse markets, in total 16142 remains of all categories related to the Great Wall are found and cataloged in this investigation.

The Great Wall stretches for thousands of kilometers, so its sections in different regions have clear local features. In Liaoning, Hebei, Tianjin and Beijing, the walls and the auxiliary facilities are usually built with bricks and stones; this might be because that these areas were the vicinities of the capital and the key defense areas and the production areas of stone materials. In Shanxi, Shaanxi, Ningxia, Inner Mongolia, Gansu and Qinghai, the walls and the related architectures were mostly built of rammed earth.

In addition to having got the accurate length, the accurate quantity of the facilities of all of the types and categories of the Ming Great Wall and other basic data, this investigation has also found some new remains related to the Ming Great Wall. A preliminary statistics shows that more than 400 localities of remains related to the Ming Great Wall have been found in this investigation. Because the data processing has not been completed yet, we can only take some examples to describe. At Dazhuangke and Haizikou in Beijing, 5 km of the Great Wall body, an iron forging workshop site, some kiln remains and quarries are newly found; in Gansu, three sections of Great Wall body and trenches, six fortresses and castles and four independent architectures are newly found, among which the special arrangement of building beacon tower in the middle of the trench is found for the first time; the courses of the sections of the Great Wall in Gulang County, Lanzhou City and some counties and districts of Baiyin City, which were confusing for hundreds of years, have been made clear; in Qian'an County, Hebei, the border tablets with inscriptions of "the west border of Yanhe Lu (route)" and "the east border of Taiping Lu" are found inlayed to the Great Wall, which marked the border between the Taiping Route and Yanhe Route both of which were under the Jizhen Defense Command. At the important passages and the easy places, many regular oval foxholes arranged in groups are found atop the stone walls. In Longguan Township, Chicheng County, a well preserved section of Great Wall body 373 m long built of untrimmed stone slabs is found. In Guyuan County, a line of beacon towers going to Kaiping Guard is found. In Liaoning, river barriers (lu he, literally "route canal") are found in Ertaizi, Kangjia, Liancheng, Longshan, Qitaizi, Santaizi, Sitaizi, Wanjiahao, Wutaizi and other townships. At Shijiagou Village in Baichangmen Township, Heishan County, eight well preserved parallel Great Wall bodies 800 m long each are found, which constructed a spectacular scene. The Damao Fortress located at Damaobao Village in Wendilou Township, Linghai City, is still preserved intact, whose bastions with curved corners are rarely seen in its counterparts of the same time. In Inner Mongolia, the section of the Great Wall newly discovered in Ordos City corrected the past opinions on the joining point of the western ends of the two courses of the Great Wall in Ningxia Defense Command: this joining point is to the north of Qingshui Garrison rather than to the north of Xingwu Garrison, which are far from each other. In Ningxia, a section of the Great Wall body 17.358 km long is found in Haiyuan County, which is the longest record in this investigation and ever before. In Qinghai, Fengtaigou Trench and Poxi Trench are found in Huangzhong County and Shijiagou Trench is found in Ledu County. In Shangxinzhuang Village, an ink-written inscription with 20 characters is found on the Great Wall body noting the labors used in the Great Wall building. In Shanxi, the Great Wall sections newly found on the southern and western ridges of Cigouying Village and Baitougou Village are all built of stone slabs; the new-found stone tablet with the introduction and map of the "New built eighteen-turn wall and the fortresses" clearly described and depicted the locations and layouts of the fortress, gate and passageway of Huangzeguan Pass. In Shaanxi, beacon towers, bastions and wall bodies buried by the desert are found in Dingbian County; in Yuyang District, Yulin City, the remains of the Great Wall bodies 76 km long in total, 33 beacon towers, 74 watchtowers, 97 bastions and 24 fortresses are found in this investigation.

Since the beginning of the Qing Dynasty, the Great Wall, having lost its original functions, was gradually abandoned and ruined, and damaged and destroyed because of natural disasters, warfare and daily lives and production activities, some sections of the Great Wall even disappeared from the ground. After the founding of the People's Republic, the protection, management and researches on the Great Wall are getting better and better. Since the 1950s, the governments and cultural institutions of all of the levels have conducted investigations to the Ming Great Wall. The sections of the Great Wall at Shanhaiguan, Badaling, Jingziguan, Jiayuguan and so on are claimed as the key ancient monuments under the state protection, provincial protection or the protection of the governments of the lower hierarchies. Some of the local governments have delimited protection scopes and development control areas for the sections of the Great Wall in their administrative areas and some of them set special agencies for the protection of these sections. Also since the 1950s, the important sections of the Great Wall, such as the Badaling, Mutianyu and Juyongguan, are maintained and amended in different scales and degrees. In 1987, the Great Wall as a whole was listed as the World Heritage; meanwhile, the governments of all of the hierarchies also intensified the punishments to the activities of damaging the Great Wall. However, seen from a comprehensive angle, the protection and management of the Great Wall are still far from the ideal situation, and this is also the reason why the preservation status is listed into the Great Wall resource investigation objects.

As an ancient monument under protection[1], it is the best for the protection and management of the Great Wall to be carried out by a single specialized agency. However, because of the historic and systematic reasons, the Ming Great Wall has been under the localized management since the very beginning, and the responsibility is on the cultural institutions or administrations of the city or county where the Great Wall goes through. A preliminary statistics shows that in the entire country, there are 183 agencies of various types involved in the management of the Ming Great Wall. The modes of the management are also diversified largely: the first is that the cultural administrative department of the local government trusts the local commission for the preservation of ancient monuments or local museums to manage the section of the Great Wall as one of the ancient monuments in its administrative area but not as a special important ancient monument. This is the majority of the management modes. Some cultural administrative departments of the local governments hire specialized managers to take care of the sections of the Great Wall in their administrative areas or sign protection contracts with the governments of the townships where the sections of the Great Wall are located, such as in some administrative areas of Hebei, Beijing and Ningxia. The third mode is that the local governments set special protection and management agencies in charge of all of the affairs of the sections of the Great Wall in these areas; these sections are usually very important and/or famous, such as Shanhaiguan and Jinshanling in Hebei, Huangyaguan in Tianjin, Juyongguan and Badaling in Beijing, Zhenbeitai, Hongshixia, Yulin Guard Garrison and Yimacheng in Shaanxi, and so on. The affiliations of these special agencies are also diversified: some are dispatched by the local government (such as Juyongguan in Beijing), some are the tourism administrative departments (such as the Administrative Bureau of Baxianshan Nature Reserve of Tianjin Municipality) and some are non-government organizations

---

[1]. Since the sixth set of the Ancient Monuments Under the State Protection, the Great Wall is listed as a single ancient monument by the State Council.

which can only carry out simple guarding and managing to the sections of the Great Wall in their administrative areas, such as the Great Wall Protection Association in Shenmu County, Shaanxi. The Ming Great Wall is distributed in the territories of ten provincial level administrative areas and some sections of it are the borders of the provincial, municipal and prefectural level administrative areas even that of counties and townships: how to manage these sections on these borders and how to distribute the responsibilities, authorities and interests are also noticeable issues in the protection and management of the Great Wall.

Delimiting the protection scope and development control area are basic requirements to the preservation and management of a historic heritage under protection. This investigation revealed that the development of the delimiting the protection scopes and development control areas of the Ming Great Wall was uneven in the relevant regions. In Liaoning, all of the sections of the Ming Great Wall claimed as the ancient monuments under the protection of the provincial and higher level have had protection scopes and development control areas; based on The Administrative Measures of Beijing Municipality for the Protection of the Great Wall and The Regulations of the Management of the Protection Scope and Development Control Areas of the Ancient Monuments under Protection in Beijing, Beijing Municipal Administration of Cultural Heritage and Beijing Municipal Commission of Urban Planning drew the temporary protection scope (500 m from the body of the Great Wall) and development control areas (the zones between 500 and 3000 m from the body of the Great Wall) for the sections of the Ming Great Wall within the Beijing Municipality; Hebei Provincial Government drew the protection scopes and development control areas in the 26 counties within Hebei Province in The Notice for the Protection Scopes and Development Control Areas of the Ancient Monuments under the State and Provincial Protections in Hebei Province, in which the protection scopes are defined as the zone 50 m from the outer margin of the base of the Great Wall, and the development control areas are defined as the zone 100 m from the outer margin of the protection scopes. The auxiliary architectures such as the beacon towers, watchtowers, pass fortresses, and so on, also had protection scopes and development control areas in the same extension. The special case is the command garrison fortress of Xuanfu Defense Command, whose protection scope was the zone 30 m from the outer margin of the wall base and development control area was the zone 70 m from the outer margin of the protection scope. In Shanxi, six localities of the Ming Great Wall remains, including the Huangzeguan Pass fortress and gate, the section of the Great Wall to the southeast of Pannao Village, the gate of Baipiguan Pass, a section of the Great Wall and a watchtower to the east of Koushang Village, have had protection scopes and development control areas drawn. In Shaanxi, ten localities of the Ming Great Wall remains distributed in Hengshan, Jingbian, Wuqi and Yuyang Counties (or Districts) have had protection scopes drawn. In Ningxia, the sections of the Great Wall in Zhongwei County and Lingwu City have had protection scopes 50 m wide from the base of the Great Wall and development control areas 100 m wide from the outer margins of the protection scopes defined. In Qinghai, only the section of the Ming Great Wall located in Qiaotou Township,

Datong County, which is claimed the ancient monument under provincial protection, has had protection scope 50 m wide from the base of the Great Wall body drawn. In Gansu, the section of the Great Wall in Yongchang County had protection scope and development control area 10 m wide from the base; that in Yongdeng County had protection scope 20 m wide from the base and development control area 150 m wide from the outer margin of the protection scope; in Jiayuguan City, the Jiayuguan Pass garrison has had the protection scope as early as in 1968; in Shandan County, the zone 15 m wide from the base of the Great Wall is defined as the protection scope and the zone 40 m wide from the outer margin of the protection scope is defined as the development control area. Up till now, only the sections of the Ming Great Wall in Tianjin Municipality and Inner Mongolia have not had protection scopes and development control areas delimited.

Erecting protection signs and building scientific records and archives are the legalized protection measures. This investigation reveals that the sections of the Great Wall listed as ancient monuments under protection of various levels all have had protection signs erected, 237 in total. However, the sections which are not listed as the protected ancient monuments have not had regular protection signs erected. Similarly, except for the points and sections of the Great Wall listed as the protected monuments, which have had records and archives, the other sections of the Great Wall almost have had no records and archives at all. One of the important objectives of this Ming Great Wall resources investigation is to build the record archives and database of the Ming Great Wall, which we believe to provide reliable data support for the protection, maintenance, display and utilization of the Great Wall.

明长城概说

李文龙

横亘于中国北方辽阔地域的明代长城，是举世公认的古代世界上规模最大、持续修筑时间最长的军事防御工程，是中国封建社会工程技术水平和劳动人民聪明智慧的集中体现。它东起辽宁省丹东市鸭绿江边的虎山，跨越湍急的河流，盘旋于险峻的山巅，绵延迤逦在贫瘠的荒漠戈壁、黄土高原，最终西止于甘肃省嘉峪关，横跨辽宁、河北、天津、北京、内蒙古、山西、陕西、宁夏、甘肃、青海10个省（自治区、直辖市），全长8851.8千米。明长城汲取了历代封建王朝长城修筑的特点，以一道或多道绵延伸展的墙体为主线，以一重或多重关堡、烽火台等军事防御设施为支撑点，点、线、面有机结合，构成了一个从中央政权通过各级军事、行政机构，联系最基层军事单位和守城戍卒的完整的、多层次的、纵深的防御体系。明长城的修筑巩固了北部边防，最大限度地保护了中原地区先进的农耕文明免遭北方游牧民族的袭扰。在发挥农耕文明与游牧文明分界线和防御蒙古贵族南下袭扰的军事屏障作用的同时，还可以看做是农耕民族和游牧民族"茶马互市"等方式的贸易场所和文化的交流带。有明一代，长城地带的民族文化、经济贸易交流从未停止和中断过，两种文明的融会贯通为多元一体的中华文明的形成和发展起到了积极作用。

今天，长城这一宏伟的古代军事防御工程虽已失去了其原有的对抗与防御的作用，但作为中华民族悠久历史和聪明智慧的见证，它不仅是"但留形胜壮山河"的历史遗迹，更是中华民族自强不息、热爱和平精神力量的象征。

一、明长城修筑的历史背景

1368年，明太祖朱元璋派大将徐达等分路北伐，进兵元大都，元顺帝率皇亲贵族等退回蒙古高原，宣告了元王朝在中原地区统治的覆灭。但残余的元朝统治集团仍有一定的实力，占有东起贝加尔湖、西至天山、北抵额尔齐斯河和叶尼塞河上游、南至今长城地带的广大区域。在西北地区有扩廓帖木儿（王保保）的18万军队，辽东有纳哈出指挥的20万大军，云南则有元宗室梁王瓦尔密的军队。蒙元集团随时都在图谋收复失去的中原地区。"元人北归，屡谋兴复。永乐迁都北平，三面近塞。正统以后，敌患日多。故终明之世，边防甚重。东起鸭绿，西抵嘉峪，绵亘万里，分地守御。"（《明史·兵志》）明太祖朱元璋一方面分派多路大军继续出塞北伐，征讨蒙元残余势力，另一方面开始全面筹划北部边防体系建设，在沿边部署军队筑城戍守成为明朝统治者的必然选择。他从中国历代封建王朝的统治策略中，总结出"内中国而外夷狄"、"固守封疆"的指导原则，对蒙元骑兵"来则击之，去则勿追，斯为上策。"（《明太祖实录·卷七十八》）明朝在北部边界建立大批都司卫所，屯兵戍守；将与蒙古高原接壤地带的民众内徙，一方面防止元朝残余势力的掠夺和袭扰，另一方面也减少蒙古骑兵内侵时边民作为内应的危险；在沿边戍守之地推行屯田，形成"三分守城，七分屯种"的制度。更为重要的是，明太祖朱元璋在长期的战争中，深知城防的重要性，他结合内地"高筑墙"的经验，在北部防线古长城的基础上修筑长城和关隘，阻挡蒙古骑兵的突袭。洪武初年，朱元璋采纳华云龙建议："自永平、蓟州、密云迤西二千余里、关隘百二十处，皆置戍守。"（《明太祖实录·卷二五二》）以后，自永乐皇帝开始，直至明朝灭亡，对北部边境长城的修筑和维护始终未曾停止。明朝先设"九边"（又称"九镇"）分地守御，后增至十三镇。长城的建筑设施不断进步，防御体系日趋完善。特别是明代隆庆至万历初年，著名将领谭纶、戚继光镇守蓟镇长城期间，对长城墙体、敌台的改建，由简单的土石墙体改为外包砖石的宽厚高墙，由简陋的骑墙墩台改建为可以"驻兵、积薪、屯粮、存储武器、御敌"的空心敌台，由互不相连的烽燧系统改建为从长城外侧经过长城沿线直至内地军镇的多路呼应、紧密相连的严密的预警系统。明长城军事防御体系布局合理，战斗生活设施齐备，后勤供应得到有效保障，极大提高了长城的军事防御能力，达到了中国古代长城修筑的高峰。

二、"九边"军事防御体系的建立

明长城所经过的区域，属于东亚大陆第二阶梯与第三阶梯之间的过渡地带，地形地貌复杂多样。明长城从辽宁省鸭绿江边的山地丘陵开始，跨越辽河平原，沿辽西走廊北侧努鲁尔虎山、医巫闾山，连接京津冀北部的燕山山地、阴山余脉，西经内蒙古高原南缘，斜跨黄土高原北部，抵宁夏贺兰山和甘肃的黄河之滨，过黄河后向西经过河西走廊的荒漠和绿洲边缘，止于茫茫戈壁上的嘉峪关。长城所经过的地带，大体属于高原—山地—平原地形的过渡带。东段大体与400毫米降雨等值线走向一致，属半干旱半湿润气候；西段则属降水量200毫米以下的干旱荒漠地区。

长城既是人类历史上持续修筑时间最长的军事防御工程，本身就是一条有形的文化界线，是自然环境和历史文化传统相结合的产物，是草原游牧和定居农耕的分野。《易经》曰："王公设险，以守其国。"东汉蔡邕曾说："天设山河，秦筑长城，汉起塞垣；所以别内外，殊异俗也。"长城所经过地区复杂多样的自然地理环境，使它自两千多年前的春秋战国时期开始，就成为北方地区的农牧交会带，即大体上以长城为界限，长城以南属农耕文明区，长城以北属游牧文明区。生产、生活方式的不同，使得以畜牧业为主的游牧民族，在日常生活资料如粮食、布匹、食盐、茶叶、工具等方面不得不依赖以农耕为主的农业民族，而农耕民族也需要马匹、牛羊等牲畜和皮革制品。当双方本应平衡对等的经济贸易交流变得不公平时，矛盾与冲突就变得不可避免。战斗力相对处于劣势的农耕民族，在组织制度、经济基础、人数上占有优势，统治者可以调集举国之力来构建边境的军事防御工程。经济、文化制度上的优势与军队作战能力的相对弱势，促使各封建王朝统治者采取"别内外"和"设险，以守其国"的边疆防御方略，使长城的修筑代代延续。在中国两千多年的封建社会中，农耕民族与游牧民族的冲突与融合、战争与贸易、交往与隔绝交错出现，既是人类适应自然环境的必然选择，也是民族与民族之间相互依存的必然结果。

明代276年的历史中，北部边防体系的建设始终没有间断，"九边"军事防区的设置渐次形成。古代长城绵延万里，地域辽阔，自然地理形势复杂多样，为更好地构建军事防御体系，历代封建王朝很早就认识到军事防区划分的重要性。战国时期在北部与游牧民族接壤地区，秦置陇西郡、上郡，赵置云中、雁门、代郡，燕置上谷、渔阳、右北平、辽西、辽东郡，可视为军事防区划分的先声。北魏时期长城沿线设"六镇"，开创了分段管理、分区防御的新格局。金代长城沿线设西北路、西南路、临潢路、东北路四路招讨使。明代"九边"的设立正是在此基础上出现的。

据《明史·兵志》记载："初设辽东、宣府、大同、延绥四镇，继设宁夏、甘肃、蓟州三镇，而太原镇总兵治偏头，三边制府驻固原，亦称二镇，是为九边。"《明史·地理志》记载："其边陲要地，称重镇者九，曰辽东，曰蓟州，曰宣府，曰大同，曰榆林，曰宁夏，曰甘肃，曰太原，曰固原。"嘉靖二十九年（1550年），增设真保镇（又称保定镇），管辖太行山区的长城关隘。次年，为护卫明代皇陵十三陵的安全，又从蓟镇西南部划出昌镇（明刘效祖《四镇三关志·卷一·建置考·真保镇建置、昌镇建置》）。万历二十三年（1595年），由固原镇分出临洮镇。万历四十六年（1618年），由蓟镇东部划出山海镇。因此，后期又有"九边十三镇"之说。"九边"建镇的时间，史家歧义颇多，尚无定论。据赵现海博士的专著《明代九边军镇体制研究》考证，甘肃镇设于洪武二十五年（1382年），宣府镇设于永乐七年（1409年），大同镇、辽东镇设于永乐十二年（1414年），宁夏镇设于宣德元年（1426年），蓟镇设于宣德三年（1428年），延绥镇设于天顺二年（1458年），固原镇初名陕西镇，设于天顺三年（1459年），弘治十八年（1505年）移镇固原，山西镇（又名三关镇）设于嘉靖二十一年（1542年）。

辽东镇长城东起辽宁省丹东虎山的鸭绿江边，西止于绥中县吾名口。设镇守总兵官1人，协守副总兵1人，分守参将5人，游击将军8人，守备5人。镇城2座：辽阳、广宁（今北镇县城），路城3座，卫城9座，所城12座，堡城121座。

蓟镇长城东起河北省山海关老龙头渤海岸边，西止于北京市怀柔区的其连口关（今莲花池）。设镇守总兵官1人，协守副总兵3人，分守参将11人，游击将军6人，守备8人。镇城1座，路城12座，关城、堡城约270座。

昌镇长城东起北京市怀柔区慕田峪东界与蓟镇长城相接，西南止于河北省怀来县水头村西南永定河北岸挂枝庵（今挂子庵）。设镇守总兵官1人，分守参将3人，游击将军2人，守备10人。镇城1座，路城3座，关城、堡城约74座。

真保镇长城北起北京市门头沟区沿河城西北永定河南岸的沿河口，南端止于太行山区的河北省沙河市、武安市交界的数道岩口。设镇守总兵官1人，分守参将4人，游击将军6人，守备7人。路城3座，关

城、堡城约300座。

宣府镇长城东起北京市延庆县四海冶口南，西止于河北省怀安县与山西省天镇县交界的西洋河堡西北的镇口台。设镇守总兵官1人，协守副总兵1人，分守参将7人，游击将军3人，守备31人。镇城1座，路城8座，关城、堡城约74座。

大同镇长城东起山西省天镇县与河北省怀安县交界的西洋河堡镇口台与宣府镇长城相接，西止于偏关县东北丫角山。设镇守总兵官1人，协守副总兵1人，分守参将9人，游击将军2人，守备39人。镇城1座，路城8座，关城、堡城约100余座。

山西镇长城西起山西省河曲县黄河东岸石梯子堡，东止于灵丘县牛邦口与真保镇相接。设镇守总兵官1人，协守副总兵1人，分守参将6人，游击将军1人，守备13人。镇城1座，路城6座，关城、堡城约100余座。

延绥镇长城东起内蒙古自治区准格尔旗龙口乡大占村黄河西岸保河台（原属陕西省府谷县），隔黄河与山西省河曲县山西镇长城相对，西止于陕西省定边县定边营村与宁夏回族自治区盐池县（旧名花马池）交界处。设镇守总兵官1人，协守副总兵1人，分守参将6人，游击将军2人，守备11人。镇城1座，路城3座，关城、堡城约60座。

宁夏镇长城东起陕西省定边县定边营西北与宁夏回族自治区盐池县交界处，西止于宁夏回族自治区中卫市南长滩村黄河南岸与甘肃省靖远县交界处。设镇守总兵官1人，协守副总兵1人，分守参将4人，游击将军3人，守备3人。镇城1座，路城5座，关城、堡城约38座。

甘肃镇长城东端起点有二：一为甘肃省兰州市安宁区沙井驿与安宁堡村之间；一为甘肃省景泰县、古浪县交界处的老虎城堡。西止于甘肃省嘉峪关南讨赖河北岸。设镇守总兵官1人，协守副总兵1人，分守副总兵1人，分守参将4人，游击将军4人，守备11人。镇城1座，路城5座，关城、堡城约87座。

固原镇长城东起陕西省定边县姬塬乡饶阳村西陕西省、甘肃省、宁夏回族自治区三省交界处，西端止点有二：一位于甘肃省兰州市安宁区沙井驿与安宁堡村之间，与甘肃镇长城相接；一为甘肃省景泰县西北松山村西北双墩子。设镇守总兵官1人，协守副总兵1人，分守副总兵1人，分守参将5人，游击将军4人，守备8人。镇城1座，路城5座，关城、堡城约55座。

临洮镇长城于万历二十三年（1595年）由固原镇西段划出，包括兰州卫、河州卫、洮州卫、岷州卫、阶州守御千户所、文县守御千户所，即原来固原镇河州路、兰州路长城辖境。东端起于兰州路一城堡的大狼沟墩（今甘肃省榆中县青城附近），西端止于甘肃镇长城东端起点之一的甘肃省兰州市安宁区沙井驿与安宁堡村之间。万历二十七年（1599年），原属固原镇的红水河堡、三眼井堡属临洮镇管辖，长城西端北移至松山双墩子。

山海镇长城于万历四十六年（1618年）由蓟镇划出东协的山海路、石门路、燕河路、建昌路（原台头路）而设立。东端仍为山海关老龙头，西端止于迁安市白羊峪关。

"九边"军事管理体系大致相同。每镇设镇守总兵官1人，为防区最高军事指挥官，驻守镇城。下设协守副总兵1人（蓟镇为3人）。镇下设若干路，路设分守参将1人，驻守路城或重要关堡。每路一般辖2卫，卫设守备1人，驻守卫城。每卫辖5个千户所，所设千总1人，驻守所城。每千户所辖10个百户所，所设把总1人，驻守所城。每百户所又辖2个总旗，各设总旗官1人，总旗又设5小旗。此外，各镇还设游击将军若干名，职位稍低于参将，驻镇城或指定关堡，受镇守总兵、巡抚调遣。镇统领士兵几万至十几万不等，路统领士兵约1.2万人，卫统军约5600人，所统军约1120人，堡城驻军约112人。总旗约50人，小旗约10人。游击统军约数千人。

三、明长城建筑结构和防御体系

长城是中国古代建立于中原地区的封建王朝为互相防御以及抵御北方游牧民族的侵扰而修筑的以连续、不封闭的高墙为主体，并与关隘、城堡、敌台、烽火台等设施紧密结合的长达数百至数千公里的军事防御工程。明长城的建筑体系依次为墙体和附属设施（敌台、马面、障墙、暗门、马道、排水孔等）、关城、堡城、烽火台以及其他与长城防御有关的设施（挡马墙、壕沟、品字窖、砖瓦窑、采石场、居住址、碑刻题记等）。

墙体是长城防线设施中最重要的部分，它直接承担着阻挡游牧骑兵突袭的重任。长城所经过的地区，地形、地势、地质条件多样，包括山地、平原、高原、河谷、荒漠、戈壁，因此在长城修筑材料的选择上"就地取材"；在地形的选择上"因地制宜"。古人概括为"因边山险，因河为固"、"因地形，用险制塞"的修筑原则，充分保证了长城的防御效果。

明代之前的长城墙体以石砌墙、土墙和土石混砌墙为主，间或有土坯墙、木障墙，还有山势险峻之处以山为险的"山险"或经过人工加工的"斩崖——修坡式山险墙"。明代隆庆至万历初年，谭纶、戚继光对蓟镇长城墙体进行了改建，墙体设置随地势平险、取材难易、防御重点不同而异，重要地段内外双重甚至多重墙体，以增加防御纵深，并由简单的土石墙体改为外包砖石的宽厚高墙，墙体加筑敌台、马面、障墙、垛口墙、射孔、瞭望孔、排水孔、暗门等设施，达到了古代长城修筑的高峰。凡在平原或要隘之处墙体修筑得十分高大坚固，在高山险峻处则较为低矮狭窄，以节约人力和费用，一些最为陡峻无法修筑的地方，采取修建"山险"、"山险墙"的办法。

石砌墙体主要分布在辽东镇、蓟镇、宣府镇、昌镇、真保镇、山西镇，大部分属于三等边墙。可分为毛石干垒和白灰勾缝两种类型，所用石料有未经打制的毛石、片石和经过打制的条石、块石，墙芯有石砌和土石混砌，外包较规整，用经过打制的块石、毛石包砌，墙体收分明显，剖面呈梯形。顶部有石砌或砖砌垛口、女墙、瞭望孔、排水沟等，可细分为石砌平顶（顶面较宽）、石砌封顶（顶面较窄）、石砌圆顶三种形式。土墙分为夯土、堆土两种，前者指以黄土或黄沙土夯打版筑，后者指将泥土堆积成墙，略经拍打，多在壕堑内外两侧，主要分布在大同镇、延绥镇、宁夏镇、固原镇、甘肃镇，宣府镇和辽东镇也有部分夯土墙体，西北地区往往在墙体内夹杂红柳、芦苇等；有平顶、封顶两种，部分有夯筑的垛口墙、瞭望孔，收分明显，剖面呈梯形或圆锥形。砖墙是指在石砌墙芯、夯土墙芯、土石混砌墙芯外侧包砌青砖，出现于明代中后期，主要分布在蓟镇，其他军镇比较少见。砖墙多位于平川之地、河谷地带、山谷沟口的关城周围，其中双面包砖者为一等边墙，单面（外侧）包砖者为二等边墙。墙体高约7~8米，底部宽约6~7米，顶部宽约4~5米，收分明显，剖面呈梯形。条石砌基，单面或双面包砖，顶面较平坦，海墁青砖，部分地段呈阶梯状，可行人马；大部分有登城步道、暗门，以供守城士卒上下；顶部内侧有女墙，外侧有垛口墙，石砌或砖砌；垛口墙上部设有瞭望孔，下部有射孔和礌石孔、排水沟和出水石嘴等。蓟镇长城重要地段墙体顶部，还建有横向障墙，墙身有射孔；墙体外侧缓坡和易于攀爬处还有挡马墙，多以毛石垒砌。延绥镇、固原镇、甘肃镇除长城墙体外，部分地段还修筑了壕堑。山险墙可以分为斩崖式和修坡式两种类型。斩崖所处地段多山势陡峭，对山体两侧的峭壁略加修整，直接作为墙体；修坡是将山坡地势平缓的外侧向下削挖，形成直而陡的断壁，然后紧贴其顶端或铲削或垒砌矮墙，与山坡形成平台。

墙体之上，明代普遍增筑马面和敌台。马面平面呈方形或半圆形，依附于墙体外侧，与墙体等高，顶部一周筑垛口，起御敌、报警作用。敌台原为骑墙墩台，是突出于墙体的高台，有实心和空心两种。戚继光镇守蓟镇长城时，发明了空心敌台。"先年边城低薄、倾圮，间有砖石小台，与墙各峙，势不相救。军士暴立暑雨霜雪之下，无所藉庇，军火器具，如临时起发，则运送不前，如收贮墙上，则无可藏处，敌势众大，乘高四射，守卒难立，一堵攻溃，相望奔走，大势突入，莫之能御。今见空心敌台，尽将通人马冲处堵塞，其制高三四丈不等，周围阔十二丈，有十七八丈不等者，凡冲处数十步或一百步一台，缓处或四五十步或二百余步不等者为一台，两台相应，左右相救，骑墙而立。造台法：下筑基与边墙平，外出一丈四五尺有余，内出五尺有余，中层空豁。四面箭窗，上层建楼橹，环以垛口，内卫战卒，下发火炮，外击敌人，敌矢不能及，敌骑不敢近。"（戚继光《练兵实纪杂记》）敌台石砌、黄土夯筑、砖砌，可分为实心高台和空心高台两种类型，平面呈正方形或圆形，剖面呈梯形；谭纶、戚继光在蓟镇创建的空心梯柱式敌台类型多样，平面呈正方形或长方形，剖面为梯形，条石砌基，夯土或土石混筑台芯，外包青砖；顺长城墙体方向开1~2个券门，四壁设箭窗、射孔等；下层为台芯；中层为正方形或长方形券室，各券室有通道相连，通道内有登顶台阶或开天井通往台顶；上层为顶面，海墁青砖，四周有垛墙、瞭望孔、吐水嘴等，部分中间有楼橹（铺房）。依中层券室形制分为单券室木梁柱结构平顶式、单券室无通道式、单券室三通道式、双券室三通道式、三券室三通道式等。空心敌台、马面的设置，将长城的防御功能发挥到了顶峰，是长城墙体防御功能科学性、合理性的完美结合。

关堡包括关城和堡城，在长城防御体系中，是守防和屯兵的中心。关城是万里长城防线上最为集中的防御据点，是出入长城的通道。大者称城，小者称口。关城设置的位置至关重要，均是选择在有利防守的地形处，是长城防守的重点，同时还收到以极少的兵力抵御强大入侵者的效果，有极冲、次冲之分。关城与长城是一体，城墙建砖砌拱券门，上筑城楼和箭楼。一般关城都建两重或数重，其间用砖石墙连接成封闭的城池，有的关城还筑有瓮城、角楼、水关或翼城，城内建登城马道，以备驻屯军士及时登城守御。堡城即屯兵城，是明代都司卫所制度的载体，按等级分为镇城、路城、卫城、所城和堡城，按照距离长城的远近又可分为前线军堡、后方屯军堡、游击堡。根据防御体系和兵制要求配置在长城内侧，间有设于墙外者。砖砌城墙，开一至四门，外设马面、角楼、护城河，有些根据防御需要在城门外建瓮城，城内按级别有衙署、营房、民居和寺庙，街道有十字街、井字街、丰字街、丁字街、一字街等，周长从14000米至200余米不等。河北省、山西省长城沿线，重要地段的关城、堡城合二为一。关城、堡城驻军按等级不同，从十几万人至一百余人不等，占地面积较大的堡城多为囤积粮草、军械、马匹等物资的后勤中枢。

烽火台作为传递军情的设施，很早就已出现，称烽燧、烽堠，明代又称烟墩、墩台，多建于长城内外的高山顶、易于瞭望的岗阜或道路折转处。"昼则举烽，夜则举火"。（《墨子·号令》）《墨子·号令·索引》韦昭注："烽，束草之长木之端，如契皋，见敌则举烧之。燧者，积薪有难则焚之。烽主昼，燧主夜。"传递的方法是白天燃烟，夜间举火，以燃烟、举火数目的多少来传递敌军的数目和方向。到了明朝还在燃烟、举火数目的同时加放炮声，以增强报警效果。明成化二年（1466年）规定："令边堠举放烽炮，若见敌一二十人至百余人举放一烽一炮，五百人二烽二炮，千人以上三烽

三炮，五千以上四烽四炮，万人以上五烽五炮"。烽火台形制是一座孤立的夯土或砖石砌高台，大部分为实心，空心台较少，平面有正方形、长方形、圆形三种，剖面呈梯形，有小券门和登顶梯道，或以绳梯上下。少量空心烽火台形制结构略同于空心敌台。台上有守望房屋和燃放烟火的柴草、报警的号炮、硝石、硫磺等，部分烽火台四周有围墙、壕沟，以护卫守军住房、羊马圈、仓房。宁夏镇、甘肃镇、宣府镇烽火台外侧，往往设有"附燧"，少者3座，多者16座。烽火台的设置方式有四种：一是紧靠长城两侧，称"沿边烽火台"；二是向长城以外延伸，称"腹外接烽火台"；三是向内侧关城、堡城伸展联系的，称"腹内接烽火台"；四是沿交通线排列的，称"加道烽火台或路墩"。在蓟镇长城沿线烽火台近旁，还发现了火池、烟灶的遗存，内有灰烬和烟熏痕迹。

四、长城的历史作用

第一，在以冷兵器为主要战争武器的年代，以长城进行军事设防，遏制北方游牧民族的袭扰，是国家安全保障的需要，是某一时间和空间内人类生存的必然产物，其积极作用十分明显，是中华民族对古代世界文明的巨大贡献。在相当长的历史时期，长城保护了长城以南农耕文化在和平稳定的环境中得以顺利发展，乃至创造出数千年不间断的以华夏民族为主体的东方文明，这种高度发达的农业文明深刻地影响了以游牧文化（包括部分渔猎文化）为主的北方民族。长城作为"有备则制人，无备则制于人"的军事设施，从简单的城、墙结合，发展到烽堠相望、敌台林立，由点到线、由线到面，层次分明、各级各类机构有机结合的严密的防御体系，为中国军事科学的进步增添了全新的内容。明代长城高大宽厚的墙体、设计合理的敌台，有效地抵御了北方蒙古骑兵的袭扰。长城"九边"防御体系不

仅突出了主要防御方向，而且加强了侧翼、纵深和后方的保护。这种防御布势，不仅着眼于敌人从正面的进攻，而且考虑了敌人组织战略迂回的可能，是比较缜密的。

第二，长城对中华民族经济文化的发展提供了保障。长城的外在形态是军事对峙，本质却是对国家利益的守护。游牧民族的掳掠，给农耕地区的人民造成许多灾难和痛苦，自然也影响到一个国家的安全与稳定。长城作为一种势力范围的标志，显示着某种战略优势，构成了一种对敌人的威慑。屯田与徙民戍边，在两千多年的封建王朝历史中，一直是管辖边疆地区的有效手段。而正是有了长城及驻军的管理监护，长城非但没有割裂各民族间的联系，反而更加有利于边地经济的发展和各民族之间有序交往与文化趋同。还可以把它看作确定边防贸易的口岸，予以集中管理、约束的一种有效的方式。大量驻军的存在，带来了中原先进的耕作制度与生产方式，军马的饲养、武器的制造、军需物资和生活物资的供给、驿路系统的开通、边地学校的开办等，从多方面促进了边境地区经济的繁荣和各民族间文化的交流与渗透。纵观两千多年中国北方边疆历史，冲突终归是暂时的，游牧经济与农耕经济的互补性（以马市为代表），"华夷兼利"的贸易原则，为边地贸易提供了广大市场。如今沿长城一线不少称为"口"的城镇，都是基于边境贸易而逐渐发展起来的。

第三，长城对中华民族统一的多民族国家的形成与巩固做出过积极贡献。在漫长的历史发展过程中，比较固定的疆域形成，终究要以一种文化传统的形态表现出来。军事占领与控制，则是走向这一过程的第一步，长城以及依附于长城伸展开的各种军事建筑，具备控驭国土的辐射功能。只有当经济文化存在取代了孤立的军事存在的时候，疆域的概念才能够初步形成。明代多种经济文化因素相互作用下形成的北方长城文化带，随着畜牧业、农业、商业贸易的发展，最终融入了中华文化的主体。长城的存在，见证了中华民族疆域发展的历史进程。同时，随着北方长城地带各民族经济文化交流的增多，各民族之间的对立与隔阂渐渐消除，推动了民族融合的发展。

现在，长城这一前后修建了近两千年的古代工程，作为中华民族两千五百年生存、进化、发展的历史见证，虽然早已失去了它原来的功用，但它作为古代世界上最伟大工程之一，仍然巍然屹立在祖国大地上，使祖国的壮丽山河更为壮丽。长城留给后人的思考，远远超过它本身的内涵与价值。长城在当代，不应当仅是"但留形胜壮山河"的历史遗存，更要在中华民族迈向现代化的过程中发挥更大的作用。

A Brief Introduction to the Ming Great Wall

Li Wenlong

Lying across the northern China, the Ming Great Wall is recognized as the largest and the longest-lasting military fortification project in ancient world. It is the concentrated embodiment of the engineering technological level and the wisdom of the Hard-working people of ancient China. Started from the Hushan Hill of Dandong, Liaoning Province on the bank of Yalu River, crossing the rapid rivers, winding along the steep mountain ridges and stretching on the deserts and loess plateau and ended at the Jiayuguan Pass in Gansu Province, the Ming Great Wall goes through Liaoning, Hebei, Tianjin, Beijing, Inner Mongolia, Shanxi, Shaanxi, Ningxia, Qinghai and Gansu, totally ten provinces and autonomous regions by a full length of 8858.8 km. The Ming Great Wall absorbed the features of the Great Walls built in the past periods, and designed a complete, multifaceted and in-depth fortification system from the central government via the military and administrative agencies of all ranks to the military units of the basic level even a warrior with one or more layers of walls as the main stem, the pass forts with watchtowers and beacon towers and one or more layers of enclosing walls as the strongholds and the organic assemblages of these lines, points and areas. The Ming Great Wall reinforced the northern frontier and protected the agricultural society from the harasses of the nomadic tribes in the northern steppes. In addition to the border of agricultural and nomadic zones and the military fortification preventing the Mongol harasses, the Ming Great Wall also played the roles as the trading center of the "Tea-horse Market" and the cultural communication center between the agricultural and nomadic peoples. In the entire Ming Dynasty, the cultural and economic interchanges across the Great Wall have never stopped or interrupted, the merging and fusing of the two civilizations through which did positive work for the formation and development of the Chinese Civilization as a pluralistic integration.

Today, Great Wall has lost its original function as the confrontation and fortification barrier, but as the evidence of the long history and the profound intelligence of the Chinese people, it is not only the historic monument to "make the landscape more spectacular" but also the spiritual symbol of the self-encouraging and peace-loving Chinese people.

1. The Historic Background of the Construction of the Ming Great Wall

In 1368, Zhu Yuanzhang, the Emperor Taizu of the Ming Dynasty, dispatched Xu Da and other generals to lead northern expedition against the Yuan Dynasty and occupied Dadu (Khanbaliq, the capital of the Yuan Dynasty, present-day Beijing), which claimed the downfall of the ruling of the Yuan Dynasty in the Central Plains. However, the remnant of the Yuan ruling group still had strong strength and still controlled the vast area from Lake Baikal in the east, Tianshan Mountains in the west, the upper reaches of Rivers Yenisei and Irtysh in the north and the Great Wall zone in the south. In the Northwest, Wang Baobao (Köke Temür) had an army of 180,000 men; in Liaodong, Nahachu had an army of 200,000 men; in Yunnan, Basalawarmi, the Prince of Liang of the Yuan Dynasty, was still controlling the region. The driven out Mongol ruling group was closely watching the chance to regain the lost Central Plains. It is noted in Bing zhi (the Treatises on military affairs) of the History of Ming that "the Yuan people retreated to the North, but they were planning to turn back day in and day out. Yongle (Emperor Chengzu of the Ming Dynasty) moved the capital to Beiping which was pressed by the frontiers from three sides. Since the Zhengtong Era (1436-1449), the threat was getting heavier and heavier. So in the entire Ming Dynasty, frontier defense was a heavy task. From Yalu (River) to Jiayu (Pass), (the Great Wall) winded for over ten thousand li as the fortification to guard against the Mongols." Zhu Yuanzhang ordered his generals to chase the remnant Yuan forces and began to design the frontier defense system and to assign troops on the frontier zone. From the ruling strategies of the past dynasties, he got the conclusive principles of guarding against the Mongol cavalries that "when they come, counterattack; when they flee, chase not (Veritable records of Emperor Taizu, vol. 78)." The Ming court established many regional military commissions and garrisons along the course of the Great Wall, migrated the residents nearby the Great Wall to the hinterland to prevent them from being sacked and harassed by the Mongols as well as from working as spies for the enemies. Meanwhile, the military farms were also set along the garrisoned zones and the rule of "three tenth of the manpower was on duty and seven tenth of that was on farm" was formed. Moreover, Zhu Yuanzhang clearly knew the importance of walled forts in the defense affairs, he adopted Hua Yunlong's suggestion of "to build 120 passes and forts in the over two thousand li westward from Yongping (present-day Lulong), Jizhou and Miyun to guard the Great Wall (Veritable records of Emperor Taizu, vol. 252)." Since then, the building and maintaining of the Great Wall along the northern frontiers were not stopped until the downfall of the Ming Dynasty. The Ming court set the "Nine Defense Commands (also known as Nine Defense Areas, later increased to Thirteen Defense Commands)" to station on the important points along the Great Wall. The architecture and defense system was gradually perfected, especially in the Longqing through the early Wanli Eras (1567-1587), when Tan Lun and Qi Jiguang, who were famous generals, were in charge of the Jizhen Defense Command on the Great Wall. They directed and supervised large-scale modification of the walls and watchtowers: from the simple stone and earth wall to the thick and high wall lined with stones and bricks, and from the solid towers to the hollow buildings in which soldiers could be hidden, firewood, grains and weapons could be stored and through which the enemies could be counterattacked. The isolated beacon towers were re-modified into swift early-warning system with many backup routes from far outside the Great Wall via the garrisons and forts to the hinterland until the commanding centers. The fortification systems of the Ming Great Wall were reasonably arranged with complete fighting and living facilities and reliable logistic supports so that the defense ability of the Great Wall was raised to the climax of the military defense architecture of ancient China.

2. The Establishment of the Military Defense System of the "Nine Defense Commands"

The zone through which the Ming Great Wall goes is on the transitional area between the second terrace and the third terrace of the East Asian Continent, which has complicated terrains and geomorphic features. From the hilly areas on the bank of Yalu River, going westward across the Liaohe Plain, climbing onto the Nulu'erhu Mountains and Yiwulü Mountain on the north end of the Liaoxi Corridor and the Yanshan and Yinshan Mountains in the north of Beijing, Tianjin and Hebei, stretching along the south margin of the Inner Mongolian Plateau, the north part of the Loess Plateau, then climbing onto the Helan Mountains and going on the bank of the Yellow River in Gansu Province; after crossing the Yellow River, going westward via the deserts and oases in the Hexi Corridor, the Great Wall ends its journey at Jiayuguan Pass on the Gobi Desert. Generally, the Great Wall is going through the transitional zones between the plateaus, mountains and plains. Its eastern section is roughly overlapping with the annual isohyet of 400 mm, which is the half-arid and half-humid climate area; its western section was in the arid and desert areas where the annual rainfall is lower than 200 mm.

The Great Wall is not only the longest-lasting military fortification construction but also a visible cultural borderline; it is the product of the blending of the natural environments and historic and cultural traditions and the divide of the nomadic and agricultural economies. It is written in Yi jing (the Book of changes) that "the kings and dukes manage the dangerous places to protect their states." Cai Yong, a writer in the Eastern Han

Dynasty, has written that "the Nature created the mountains and rivers; the Qin and Han Dynasties built the Great Wall and the forts and passes to separate the inner and outer and to distinguish the different customs." Because of its diversified natural geographic environment, the zone in which the Great Wall goes became the interaction area of the agricultural and nomadic cultures and economies. The different subsistence modes and lifestyles of the peoples on the two sides of the Great Wall made them need the products of each other. The nomads to the north of the Great Wall needed the grains, textiles, salt, tea and tools produced in the agricultural society; the farmers also needed livestock such as horses, oxen and sheep and leather products from the nomadic people. When the trade and interchange, which should have been fair and mutual beneficial, became unfair, the confrontation and conflict would be unavoidable. The agricultural people, whose fighting capability was weaker than that of nomadic people but the organizing capability, economic foundation and population were all in superiority, could levy the resource of the whole country to construct the fortification system. This superiority in economy, culture and political system and the inferiority in fighting capability made the rulers of the Central Plains apply the strategy of "manage the dangerous places to protect their states" and continue the construction of the Great Walls for thousands of years. During the feudalist society of over 2,000 years in China, the alternative occurring of the conflicting and fusing, fighting and trading, communicating and separating between the agricultural and nomadic peoples are the results of the adaptation of the peoples to the natural environment and the interdependence among the different ethnic groups and peoples with different subsistence types.

In the 276 years of the Ming Dynasty, the construction of the northern frontier fortification system was never interrupted and the defense zones of the "Nine Defense Commands" were formed gradually. In the vast land through which the Great Wall goes, the natural geographies are sharply diversified; to build military fortification system as good as possible, the rulers of the ancient Central Plains had known the importance of the zoning of the military defense areas. In the Warring-States Period, the Qin State set Longxi and Shang Commanderies, the Zhao State set Yunzhong, Yanmen, Dai Commanderies, the Yan State set Shanggu, Yuyang, Youbeiping, Liaoxi and Liaodong Commanderies, which could be seen as the forerunners of the division of military defense areas. In the Northern Wei Dynasty, along the Great Wall route, the "Six Frontier Towns" were set, which started the new mode of sectional administration and sectional defense systems. In the Jin Dynasty, the bandit-suppression commissions of the Northwest Route, Southwest Route, Linhuang Route and Northeast Route were arranged along the Great Wall. The "Nine Defense Commands" system of the Ming Dynasty was evolved from these defense settings.

According to the Bing zhi (the Treatises on military affairs) of the History of Ming, "at first, the four defense commands which were Liaodong, Xuanfu, Datong and Yansui were set, followed by Ningxia, Gansu and Jizhou Defense Commands; in addition, the Piantou Pass was governed by the regional commander of Taiyuan Defense Command and the general supervisor of Yansui, Ningxia and Gansu Defense Commands was stationed in Guyuan, so Taiyuan and Guyuan were also called as 'defense commands' and the name of the 'Nine Defense Commands' was given as their collective name." In the twenty-ninth year of Jiajing Era (1550), Zhenbao (also know as Baoding) Defense Command was set to supervise the forts and passes of the Great Wall in the Taihang Mountains. In the next year, to ensure the safety of the imperial mausoleums, the southwestern part of Jizhou Defense Command was separated as the Chang Defense Command. In the twenty-third year of Wanli Era (1595), Lintao Defense Command was separated from Guyuan Defense Command. In the forty-sixth year of Wanli Era (1618), the eastern part of Jizhou Garrison was separated as the Shanhai Garrison. Therefore, in the later Ming Dynasty, another general name of "Nine Defense Commands and Thirteen Defense Areas" was also known. To date, the concrete dates of the establishments of the Nine Defense Commands are still in controversy. As Dr. Zhao Xianhai's dissertation titled as A study of the nine frontier fortification system of the Ming Dynasty, Gansu Defense Command was set in the twenty-fifth year of Hongwu Era (1392), Datong and Liaodong Defense Commands were set in the twelfth year of Yongle Era (1414), Ningxia Defense Command was set in the first year of Xuande Era (1426), Ji (Jizhou) Defense Command was set in the third year of Xuande Era (1428); Yansui Defense Command was set in the second year of Tianshun Era (1458), Guyuan Defense Command, which was called Shaanxi Defense Command at the very beginning, was set in the third year of Tianshun Era, and transferred to Guyuan in the eighteenth year of Hongzhi Era (1505); Shanxi (also known as Sanguan -- Three-pass) Defense Command was set in the twenty-first year of Jiajing Era (1542).

The section of the Great Wall guarded by Liaodong Defense Command was started from the eastern end of the whole Great Wall on the bank of Yalu River and ended at Wumingkou Pass in Suizhong County in the west. It was headed by one zongbing (regional commander), under whom one regional vice commander, five canjiang (assistant regional commanders), eight youji jiangjun (mobile corps commanders) and five shoubei (commandants) were assigned. In this section, there were two command garrisons which were Liaoyang and Guangning (present-day Beizhen County seat), three lu cheng (route garrisons), nine wei cheng (guard garrisons), twelve suo cheng (battalion barracks) and 121 fortresses.

The section of the Great Wall guarded by Ji (Jizhou) Defense Command was started from the coast of Bohai Sea at Laolongtou, Shanhaiguan Pass in Hebei Province in the east and ended at Qiliankou Pass (present-day Lianhuachi) in Huairou County, Beijing in the west. It was headed by one zongbing (regional commander), under whom three regional vice commanders, eleven canjiang (assistant regional commanders), six youji jiangjun (mobile corps commanders) and eight shoubei (commandants) were assigned. In this section, there were one command garrison, twelve route garrisons and about 270 passes and fortresses.

The section of the Great Wall guarded by Chang Defense Command was started from Mutianyu in Huairou County, which was jointed to that of Ji Defense Command in the east, and ended at Guazhi An on the north bank of Yongding River to the southwest of Shuitou Village in Huailai County, Hebei Province in the west. It was headed by one regional commander,

under whom three assistant regional commanders, two mobile corps commanders and ten commandants were assigned. In this section, there were one command garrison, three route garrisons, and 74 passes and fortresses.

The section of the Great Wall guarded by Zhenbao Defense Command was started from Yanhekou on the south bank of Yongding River to the northwest of Yanhecheng in Mentougou District, Beijing in the north and ended at some rocky passes on the border of Shahe and Wu'an Cities, Hebei in the Taihang Mountains in the south. It was headed by one regional commander, under whom four assistant regional commanders, six mobile corps commanders and seven commandants were assigned. In this section, there were three route garrisons and about 300 passes and fortresses.

The section of the Great Wall guarded by Xuanfu Defense Command was started from the south of Sihaiye Pass in Yanqing County, Beijing in the east and ended at Zhenkoutai to the northwest of Xi Yanghepu on the border of Huai'an County, Hebei and Tianzhen County, Shanxi in the west. It was headed by one regional commander, under whom one regional vice commander, seven assistant regional commanders, three mobile corps commanders and 31 commandants were assigned. In this section, there were one command garrison, eight route garrisons and 72 passes and fortresses.

The section of the Great Wall guarded by Datong Defense Command was started from Zhenkoutai, which was jointed to that of Xuanfu Defense Command in the east, and ended at Yajiao Mount to the northeast of Pianguan County seat, Shanxi Province in the west. It was headed by one regional commander, under whom one regional vice commander, nine assistant regional commanders, two mobile corps commanders and 39 commandants were assigned. In this section, there were one command garrison, eight route garrisons and over 100 passes and fortresses.

The section of the Great Wall guarded by Shanxi Defense Command was started from Shitizipu on the east bank of the Yellow River in Hequ County, Shanxi Province in the west and ended at Niubangkou Pass in Lingqiu County, Shanxi Province, which was jointed to that of Zhenbao Defense Command, in the east. It was headed by one regional commander, under whom one regional vice commander, six assistant regional commanders, one mobile corps commander and 13 commandants were assigned. In this section, there were one command garrison, six route garrisons and over 100 passes and fortresses.

The section of the Great Wall guarded by Yansui Defense Command was started from Baohetai on the west bank of the Yellow River at Dazhan Village in Longkou Township, Jungar Banner, Inner Mongolia (which has belonged to Fugu County, Shaanxi) in the east and ended at Dingbianying Village on the border of Dingbian County, Shaanxi and Yanchi County, Ningxia in the west. It was headed by one regional commander, under whom one regional vice commander, six assistant regional commanders, two mobile corps commanders and eleven commandants were assigned. In this section, there were one command garrison, three route garrisons and over 60 passes and fortresses.

The section of the Great Wall guarded by Ningxia Defense Command was started from Dingbianying Village on the border of Dingbian County, Shaanxi and Yanchi County, Ningxia in the east and ended at Nan Changtan Village on the south bank of the Yellow River in Zhongwei City, Ningxia in the west. It was headed by one regional commander, under whom one regional vice commander, four assistant regional commanders, three mobile corps commanders and three commandants were assigned. In this section, there were one command garrison, five route garrisons and 38 passes and fortresses.

The section of the Great Wall guarded by Gansu Defense Command had two starting points in the east: one was between Shajingyi and Anningpu in Anning District, Lanzhou City, Gansu and the other was the old castle on the border of Jingtai and Gulang Counties, Gansu Province. This section was ended on the north bank of Taolai River to the south of Jiayuguan Pass in Gansu Province. It was headed by one regional commander, under whom one regional vice commander, four assistant regional commanders, four mobile corps commanders and eleven commandants were assigned. In this section, there were one command garrison, five route garrisons and 87 passes and fortresses.

The section of the Great Wall guarded by Guyuan Defense Command was started from the joint of Shaanxi, Gansu and Ningxia to the west of Raoyang Village in Jiyuan Township, Dingbian County, Shaanxi in the east; its west end has two places: the first was jointed to the Great Wall of Gansu Defense Command between the Shajingyi and Anningpu in Anning District, Lanzhou City; the second was at Shuangdunzi to the northwest of Songshan Village in Jingtai County, Gansu Province. It was headed by one regional commander, under whom two regional vice commanders (one was in the same garrison with the regional commander and the other was assigned to another place), five assistant regional commanders, four mobile corps commanders and eight commandants were assigned. In this section, there were one command garrison, give route garrisons and 55 passes and fortresses.

Lintao Defense Command was set in the twenty-third year of Wanli Era (1595) by separating the west part of the defense area of Guyuan Defense Command. It included Lanzhou Guard, Hezhou Guard, Taozhou Guard, Minzhou Guard, Jiezhou shouyu qianhu (Independent Battalion) and Wenxian Independent Battalion, which had been the defense areas of Hezhou Route and Lanzhou Route of Guyuan Defense Command. The section of the Great Wall guarded by this defense command was started at Dalanggoutun (nearby present-day Qingcheng in Yuzhong County, Gansu) in the east and ended between the Shajingyi and Anningpu in Anning District, Lanzhou City in the west, which was one of the starting points of the section guarded by Gansu Defense Command. In the twenty-seventh year of Wanli Era (1599), the Hongshuihe and Sanyanjing Forts which had been under the control of Guyuan Defense Command were reassigned to Lintao Defense Command and the west end of the Great Wall was moved northward to Shuangdunzi in Jingtai County.

Shanhai Defense Command was set in the forty-sixth year of Wanli Era (1618) by separating the east part of the defense area of Jizhou Defense Command, which were the Shanhai, Shimen, Yanhe, Jianchang (whose old name was Taitou) Routes. Its starting point in the east was still the Laolongtou of Shanhaiguan Pass and the ending point was Baiyangyu Pass in Qian'an City.

The military management systems of the Nine Defense Commands were roughly the same. Each defense command was headed by a zongbing (regional commander) headquartered in the zhen cheng (command garrison or command city). He was assisted by a fu zongbing (regional vice commander, in Jizhou Defense Command, there were three of them). The defense area of a defense command was divided into some lu (route), each of which was headed by a canjiang (assistant regional commander) headquartered in lu cheng (route garrisons) or an important pass or fortress. Generally, each route had two wei (guards) headed by a shoubei (commandant) headquartered in wei cheng (guard garrison). Each wei had five qianhu suo (battalion) each of which headed by a qianzong (battalion commander) headquartered in suo cheng (battalion barracks). Each qianhu suo had ten baihu suo (company) each of which headed by a bazong (company commander). Each baihu suo had two zongqi (platoon) each of which headed by a zongqi guan (platoon commander). Each zongqi had five qi (squad). In addition, each defense command had several youji jiangjun (mobile corps commanders), whose rank was slightly lower than that of canjiang, stationed in the command garrison or assigned to certain passes or forts waiting for the dispatching of the regional commander or xunfu (grand coordinator). A defense command leaded dozens of thousands to over one hundred thousand men, a route leaded about twelve thousand men, a guard leaded about 5600 men, a battalion, 1120 men. Each fort was stationed by about 112 men; a platoon had 50 men and a squad, 10 men. Each mobile corps commander leaded thousands of men.

3. The Construction Structure and Defense System of the Ming Great Wall

The Great Wall was military defense engineering project made by the rulers in the Central Plains to guard against the raids from the nomadic tribes in the northern steppes. The main body of the Great Wall was the linear but not enclosed long walls, reinforced by passes, forts, watchtowers, beacon towers and other facilities, the whole length of which was usually thousands of kilometers. The defense system of the Ming Great Wall consisted of the walls and the auxiliary facilities (watchtowers, bastions, blocking walls, secret doors, ramps, the draining system, etc.), the passes, the fortresses, the beacon towers and other facilities (stockades, trenches, triangle horse pitfalls, brick kilns, quarries, residential areas, monuments and inscriptions, etc.)

The wall, which directly held the responsibility of holding back the sudden attack of the cavalries of the nomadic tribes, was the most important part of the fortification system of the Great Wall. The areas through which the Great Wall passed had very diversified topographic and geologic features, including mountain and hilly lands, plains, plateaus, valleys, deserts and oases, therefore, the building materials of the Great Wall through these areas were different according to local conditions and the choices of the terrains for the Great Wall to locate were taking the best advantage of the natural topography. The ancient people concluded the principles as "using mountains and hills as walls and using rivers as moats" and "taking advantage of the terrains and building fortifications at the most dangerous places" which fully guaranteed the defending effects of the Great Wall.

The wall bodies of the Great Walls before the Ming Dynasty were mostly stone walls, rammed-earth walls or stone-earth walls, in a few places adobe walls and wood log walls, and sometimes the natural steep cliffs or artificially steepened slopes used as walls, which were called as "steep mountain walls". In the Longqing to early Wanli Eras (1567-1587), Tan Lun and Qi Jiguang managed and supervised the reconstruction of the section of the Great Wall guarded by the Ji Defense Command. The building of the walls varied according to the terrains, available materials, defending importance, and so on: at the important locations, double even multiple layers of walls were built for an in-depth defense; the walls were also built as thick ones lined with bricks or stone blocks. Across or on the walls, watchtowers, bastions, blocking walls, battlements, watching holes, machicolations, drainage system and secret doors were set, all of which represented the highest level of the Great Wall construction techniques in ancient times. At the flat and/or important locations, the walls were built high, thick and firm; at the mountain or hilly areas, the walls were built somewhat lower and narrower to save manpower and cost. In some dangerous and steep places, the natural terrains like cliffs or artificially steepened slopes were utilized in stead of walls.

The stone walls were mainly in Liaodong, Ji (Jizhou), Xuanfu, Chang, Zhenbao and Shanxi Defense Commands, most of which belonged to Grade Three walls. The stone walls could be classified into dry laid stone walls and lime-plastered stone walls. The materials were stone blocks in various statuses, such as original rocks, flakes or processed slabs. The core of the wall was built with stone or mixture of stone and earth and lined with regular stone slabs or raw rocks. The batter of the wall was clear and the cross-section of the wall was in a trapezoid shape. On the top of the wall, stone or brick battlements, parapets, watching holes and draining ditches were built; the top could also be classified into flat wide top, flat narrow top and curved top. The earth walls, which were mainly distributed in the defense areas of Datong, Yansui, Ningxia, Guyuan and Gansu Defense Commands, a few were also found in the defense areas of Xuanfu and Liaodong Defense Commands, could be classified into rammed-earth walls and piled earth walls. The former was built by ramming earth filled between the formworks and the latter was built by simply piling up the earth into walls or slightly patting, most of which were set on the two sides of the trenches. In the Northwest, the earth wall bodies were usually reinforced with wild poplar branches or reeds. On the top of the earth walls, there were sometimes rammed-earth battlements and watchtowers, and the tops were obviously narrower than the bases. The tops had wider and narrower types. The brick walls referred to the walls with stone, earth or stone-earth mixed cores and lined with bricks, which appeared in the mid to late Ming Dynasty and mainly in the defense area of Ji Defense Command but are seldom seen in other areas. The brick walls were mostly built in the flat places, the river valleys and the flanking the pass forts guarding important passages. The walls lined on both inner and outer sides were Grade One walls and only on one side (the outer side) were Grade Two walls. The walls were averagely 7-8 m high and 6-7 m thick at the base and 4-5 m at the top, the batter of wall are clear even today. The foundations of the brick walls were laid with stone planks, the tops were usually flat and paved with bricks (in some places the tops of the walls were built as steps) on which horses and troops could travel. Most of the walls had mounting steps and secret doors for the soldiers to go to the top; battlements were built on the outer side of the top and parapets on the inner side, both of which with bricks or stones. On the top of the battlements, watching holes were opened and on the bottom, machicolations for shooting or releasing stone missiles were opened, as well as draining ditches and stone draining spouts. In some important sections of the Great Wall in Ji Defense Command, transverse blocking walls with machicolations were also built on the top of the wall to counterattack the enemies having mounted the wall. On the gentler slopes and places easier to climb, stockades were built with raw rocks. In the defense areas of Yansui, Guyuan and Gansu Defense Commands, trenches were dug in addition to the walls. The "steep mountain walls" had two types: cutting cliff and steepening slope. The cutting cliff walls were located at the terrains with sharp cliffs, which were used as walls after slight modifications; the steepening slope walls were made by cutting the gentle slopes into steep cliffs and then building walls on its top or flattening the top end of the steepened cliff into a platform as the top of the wall.

In the Ming Dynasty, bastions (mamian) and watchtowers (ditai) were built on the wall bodies. The bastions were in square or semicircular plan and built on the outer side of the wall body, the top of which were the same and battlements were built on the top of the bastions for counterattacking the climbing enemies and giving alert. Watchtowers were both higher and wider than the wall body. Originally, the watchtowers were solid ones which were square or circular in plan and trapezoidal in elevation. When Qi Jiguang was in charge with the Ji Defense Command, he invented hollow watchtowers. In the chapter zaji (miscellany) of his Lianbing shiji (A practical account of troop training), Qi Jiguang wrote: "in the past, the walls of the frontier fortification were low and thin, usually collapse; the small terraces (watchtowers) were built separated from the walls and could not reinforce each other. The soldiers were exposed in the hot, cold, rainy or snowy weathers without shelters; the weapons and ammos, if sent from the rear once needed, it would not be timely available; if stored on the terrace, there would not be houses to hide them. When the enemies came in large group and shot densely, the soldiers did not have enough space to cover themselves; when a small part was seized by the enemies, the soldiers of the neighboring parts would flee one after another and the enemies breaking in could not be held back any longer. Now, the hollow watchtowers built at the key locations and passages are thirty to forty chi (10-13 m) high and one hundred and twenty (40 m) to one hundred and eighty chi (60 m) long in perimeter at the base; at the important sections, several dozens to one hundred paces (utmost 200 m) there must be a watchtower; at the sections not very important, every one hundred and fifty paces to two hundred paces (300 m to 400 m) there must be a watchtower. Two neighboring watchtowers could reinforce and cover each other. The method of building the watchtower: the base is on the same level with that of the wall; on the outer side, the watchtower should be projecting out of the wall by 15 chi (5 m) and on the inner side, 5 chi (1.7 m) or so; the middle floor is hollow with arrow windows (machicolations) on the four sides; the top floor is the guardhouse surrounded by the battlements, the soldiers stay in the top floor and the cannons are set under the battlements to fire the enemies. The arrows of the enemies could reach the soldiers and the cavalries of the enemies don't dare to approach." The hollow watchtowers invented by Tan Lun and Qi Jiguang in Ji Defense Command had many types, all of which were in rectangular or square plans and trapezoid elevation. The foundations of the watchtowers were laid with stone slabs and the first floor was filled with rammed earth or earth-stone mixture. The second floor was partitioned into some square or rectangular chambers with vaulted ceilings and linked to each other by corridors which also had steps leading to the top of the watchtower. On the walls of the second floor, one or two arched doorways were opened parallel with the direction of the Great Wall, and several machicolations were opened on each side of this floor. The top floor was paved with bricks and surrounded by battlements and watch holes and draining spouts, and some watchtowers had a guardhouse in the middle of the top. By the number and shape of the chambers in the middle floor, the watchtowers could be classified into single-chamber with timber structure and flat ceiling, single-chamber with vaulted ceiling and without corridor, single-chamber with vaulted ceiling and three corridors, double-chamber with vaulted ceiling and three corridors, three-chamber with vaulted ceiling and three corridors, and so on. The setting of hollow watchtowers and bastions fully developed the defense function of the Great Wall and integrated their functions perfectly, scientifically and rationally.

The and forts, including pass fortresses and garrisons, were the centers of guarding and stationing troops in the defense system of the Great Wall. Pass fortresses (or passes) were the passageways going through the Great Wall and the most important defense points, the larger ones of which were called "guan" and the smaller ones, "kou". The location selection of the pass fortresses was fundamentally important; all of the pass fortresses were built at the terrain favorable for defense where very few soldiers could defend the attack of strong enemies. These pass fortresses were classified into the primary key and secondary key ones. The pass fortresses were jointed to the Great Wall; the brick-built arched gates were the entrances of the Great Wall, above which the gate tower and watchtowers were built. Generally, the pass fortresses were enclosed with double or multiple layers of walls, and some pass fortresses had barbicans, corner towers, Watergates, wing forts, and so on to strengthen the defense; mounting ramps or steps were built on the inside of the walls for the soldiers to get on the wall in time. The garrisons were the carriers of the dusi (regional military commissions) wei-suo (guard-battalion) system, which were hierarchized into zhen cheng (command garrisons), lu cheng (route garrisons), wei cheng (guard garrisons), suo cheng (battalion barracks) and pu cheng (fortresses) by ranks. By the distances to the Great Wall, they could be classified into frontier forts, rear barracks and mobile corps bases. According to the fortification system and the military requirements, these garrisons were usually arranged inside the Great Wall, but there were also some of them set outside the Great Wall. These garrisons were enclosed by brick walls 14 km to 200 m in perimeter, through which one to four gates were opened, and on the walls, bastions and corner towers

were built, and moats were dug around the outside of the walls. Some of the garrisons had barbicans built around the gates. In the garrisons, official buildings, barracks, residential areas and temples were built by ranks; the streets were arranged in cross plan or multi-intersection plans, or simply one main street was going through the garrison. In some key sections of the Great Wall in present-day Hebei and Shanxi Provinces, the garrisons were built in the pass fortresses. Varying as the ranks, the troops stationed in the garrisons were from over one hundred thousand to about one hundred; the larger garrisons were usually also the logistics centers for storing grain and fodder, weapons and raising horses.

As facilities for transferring military information, beacon towers emerged very early in China. In the Ming Dynasty, they were also called smoke towers, which were usually built on the mountain tops, highlands easy for watching, and turns of the roads. It was noted in Mozi that "during the day, beacon smoke is used; in the evening, beacon fire is used." The numbers of the smoke columns or flames represented the numbers and directions of the enemies coming to attack. In the Ming Dynasty, in addition to the smoke and fire, gunfire was used to reinforce the effect of warning. In the second year of Chenghua Era (1466), a regulation was issued to define "if ten to one hundred enemies came, one beacon flame is set and one sound of cannon is fired; up to five hundred, two flames and two sounds of cannon; up to one thousand, three flames and three sounds of cannon; five thousand, four; over ten thousand, five." A beacon tower was an isolated high terrace built of rammed-earth or brick and stone, usually solid, in circular, square or rectangular plans; it had stairs for mounting, or sometimes only rope ladders. A few hollow beacon towers were built in the similar structure to that of the hollow watchtowers. On the top of the beacon tower, a guardhouse was built and firewood, signal cannon, sulfur and gunpowder were stored. Some beacon towers were enclosed by walls and ditches to protect the dwellings, horse and sheep stables and warehouses of the guarding soldiers. In the defense areas of Ningxia, Gansu and Xuanfu Defense Commands, subsidiary towers were usually set outside each beacon tower, the number of the subsidiary towers varied from three to sixteen. The setting of the beacon towers had four types: one was closely distributed along the inner and outer sides of the Great Wall; the second was lined up outwards from the Great Wall; the third was linked to the garrisons inside the Great Wall and the fourth, lined up along the traffic lines. Nearby the beacon towers along the Great Wall guarded by Ji Defense Command, hearths and smoke stoves were found, in which ashes and soot traces were still preserved.

4. The Historic Effects of the Great Wall

First, in the Cold Steel Age, building Great Wall to prevent the nomadic tribes in the northern steppes from attacking and harassing was the need of the national security and the requirement for the people to live in peace within the given temporal and spatial conditions. The Great Wall played positive roles and contributed greatly to the ancient civilizations all over the world. In a rather long history, the Great Wall protected the agricultural cultures to develop in a favorable environment and to keep the civilization from interruption for thousands of years; this highly-developed agricultural civilization also deeply influenced the nomadic (as well as some fishing -hunting) tribes in the north. As a military defense facility, the Great Wall developed from the simple walls and combinations of forts and walls to the integration of multi-level defense system consisting of watching and warning system, commanding system, supply system, reinforcing system and stationing system, and defending from points to lines and to areas, not only in width but also in depth, and added new contents to the military science development in ancient China. The thick and high walls and rationally designed watchtowers of the Ming Great Wall effectively guarded against the attacking and harassing of the Mongol cavalries from the north. The defense system of the "Nine Defense Commands" not only paid attention to the main defense directions but strengthened the protections of the flanks, depth and rear. This defense arrangement considered both the frontal invasion and the strategic outflanking of the enemies, so it was a deliberate defense design. These military strategic thoughts are worthy studying and referring for us.

Second, the Great Wall provided guarantee for the economy and culture of Chinese nationality to develop. The external look of the Great Wall was military confrontation, but its nature was the protector of the national interests. The attacking and ransacking of the nomadic tribes made havocs and sufferings to the people of the agricultural areas and also harmed the security and stability of a state power. As the sign of a sphere of power, the Great Wall showed a strategic superiority and a deterrence force against the enemies. The military farming and migration to augment the frontier defense have been effective measures for the state powers to govern the frontier areas in the over 2000 years since the unification of the Qin Dynasty. Just because of the administration of the government and the protection of the troops stationed along it, the Great Wall did not separate the peoples living on both sides of it but did favor to the development of the frontier economy and the beneficial communication and cultural converging. The Great Wall could be utilized as the given trade market which was easy to manage and regulate. The stationed troops brought the advanced cultivation system and production techniques, and the raising of the military livestock, the making and maintaining of weapons, the management of civil and military supplies, the establishing of the posting road network and the opening of frontier schools all brought about the prosperity of the frontier economy and the communication and merging of the cultures of different ethnic groups. When we comprehensively view the history of the northern frontiers in the over 2000 years, we will find that the conflicts were taking just very short times, and the complementarity of agricultural and nomadic economies and the trading principle of "beneficial to the peoples of both the Central Plains and the North Steppes" provided good condition for the frontier trades. At present, many cities and townships along the Great Wall whose names had the "kou" as the last character are evolved from the frontier trading centers which had been the pass fortresses when the Great Wall was in use.

Third, the Great Wall significantly contributed to the formation and consolidation of the Chinese Nationality as a pluralistic integration. In the long development of history, the formation of a relatively stable territory would be represented or embodied by a cultural tradition. The military occupation and control was the first step of this procedure and the Great Wall and the auxiliary facilities based on it had the radiation function of territory control. Only when the economic and cultural existences replaced the military existence, the concept of territory could be formed. The Great Wall Cultural Belt formed in the Ming Dynasty under the interactions of the multiple economic and cultural elements finally merged into the main body of the Chinese Culture along with the developments of the animal husbandry, agriculture and commercial activities. The Great Wall witnessed the historic procedure of the development of the Chinese territory. Meanwhile, along with the increasing of the economic and cultural interchanges among the ethnic groups living in the zones flanking the Great Wall, the confrontation and alienation among these peoples were gradually vanishing and the unity was developing.

Today, as the historic evidence of the surviving, evolving and developing of Chinese Nationality in the past 2500 years, the Great Wall, the ancient construction project being built for over 2000 years, has lost its original function; however, as one of the greatest artificial wonders of ancient world, it still stands on the vast territory of our nation and makes our nation's landscapes more magnificent. The considerations left by the Great Wall to us and the future people are much more than its own connotation and value. In the modern time, the Great Wall is not only a historic heritage to "make the landscape more spectacular" but will play more important roles in the progress of the Chinese Nationality to the modernization.

明 长 城 THE MING GREAT WALL

图版
Plates

墙体、自然险、壕堑
Walls, Natural Barriers and Trenches

1	2
3	

1.辽宁省宽甸县虎山长城——明长城东端起点
Hushan Great Wall, Kuandian County, Liaoning Province - the eastern starting point of the Ming Great Wall

2.辽宁省新宾满族自治县下夹河长城
Xiajiahe Great Wall, Xinbin Manchu Autonomous County, Liaoning Province

3.辽宁省凌海市龟山长城
Guishan Great Wall, Linghai City, Liaoning Province

辽宁省葫芦岛市小虹螺山长城
Xiaohongluoshan Great Wall, Huludao City, Liaoning Province

辽宁省绥中县金牛洞长城
Jinniudong Great Wall, Suizhong County, Liaoning Province

辽宁省绥中县鼓山长城
Gushan Mountain Great Wall, Suizhong County, Liaoning Province

辽宁省绥中县蔓枝草长城
Wanzhicao Great Wall, Suizhong County, Liaoning Province

辽宁省绥中县椴木冲长城
Duanmuchong Great Wall, Suizhong County, Liaoning Province

辽宁省绥中县锥子山长城
Zhuizishan Great Wall, Suizhong County, Liaoning Province

辽宁省绥中县锥子山长城
Zhuizishan Great Wall, Suizhong County, Liaoning Province

辽宁省绥中县、河北省抚宁县九门口长城
Jiumenkou Great Wall, Suizhong County, Liaoning Province / Funing County, Hebei Province

河北省秦皇岛市山海关区老龙头入海石城
Laolongtou Estuary Stone City, Shanhaiguan District, Qinhuangdao City, Hebei Province

河北省秦皇岛市山海关区三道关倒挂长城
Daogua (Hanging) Great Wall, Shanhaiguan District, Qinhuangdao City, Hebei Province

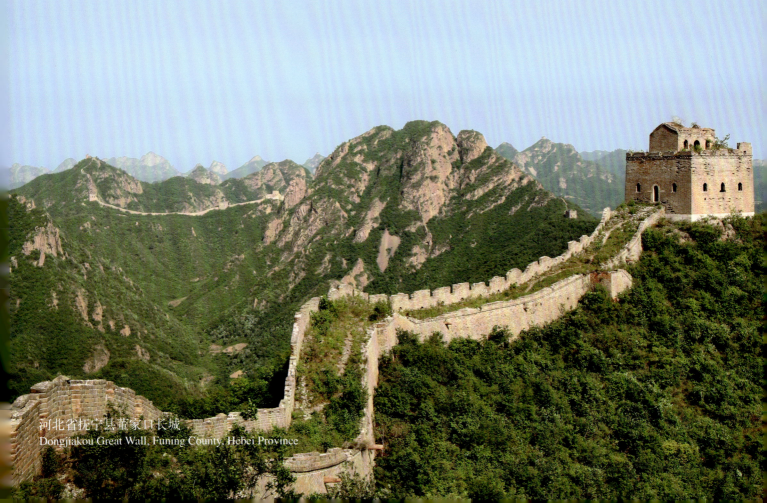

河北省抚宁县董家口长城
Dongjiakou Great Wall, Funing County, Hebei Province

河北省抚宁县花场峪长城
Huachangyu Great Wall, Funing County, Hebei Province

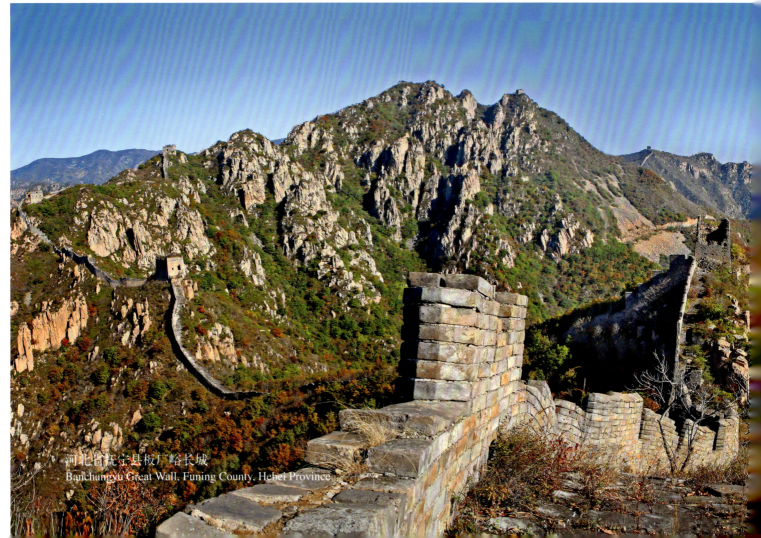

河北省抚宁县板厂峪长城
Banchangyu Great Wall, Funing County, Hebei Province

$\dfrac{1}{2}$

1~2.河北省卢龙县刘家口长城
Liujiakou Great Wall, Lulong County, Hebei Province

河北省迁安市红峪口长城
Hongyukou Great Wall, Qian'an City, Hebei Province

河北省迁安市水泉寺长城
Shuiquansi Great Wall, Qian'an City, Hebei Province

河北省迁安市白羊峪长城
Baiyangyu Great Wall, Qian'an City, Hebei Province

河北省迁安市冷口长城
Lengkou Great Wall, Qian'an City, Hebei Province

河北省迁西县大岭寨长城墙体及外侧挡马墙
Dalingzhai Great Wall and the Exterior Stockades, Qianxi County, Hebei Province

河北省迁西县西城峪长城
Xichengyu Great Wall, Qianxi County, Hebei Province

河北省迁西县榆木岭长城
Yumuling Great Wall, Qianxi County, Hebei Province

河北省唐山市迁西县喜峰口长城
Xifengkou Great Wall, Qianxi County, Hebei Province

河北省宽城县蟠龙湖长城
Panlonghu Great Wall, Kuancheng County, Hebei Province

天津市蓟县赤霞峪长城
Chixiayu Great Wall, Jixian County, Tianjin

天津市蓟县赤霞峪长城
Chixiayu Great Wall, Jixian County, Tianjin

天津市蓟县船舱峪长城
Chuancangyu Great Wall, Jixian County, Tianjin

天津市蓟县船舱峪长城
Chuancangyu Great Wall, Jixian County, Tianjin

天津市蓟县车道峪长城
Chedaoyu Great Wall, Jixian County, Tianjin

2
―
1 3

1~2.天津市蓟县黄崖关长城
Huangyaguan Pass Great Wall, Jixian County, Tianjin

3.天津市蓟县前干涧长城
Qianganjian Great Wall, Jixian County, Tianjin

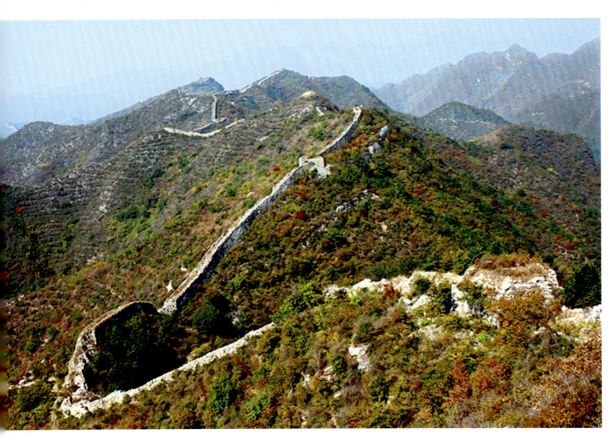

北京市平谷区红石门长城
Hongshimen Great Wall, Pinggu District, Beijing

北京市平谷区彰作长城
Zhangzuo Pass Great Wall, Pinggu District, Beijing

1.北京市平谷区彰作长城
Zhangzuo Pass Great Wall, Pinggu District, Beijing

2.北京市平谷区黄松峪长城
Huangsongyu Great Wall, Pinggu District, Beijing

3.北京市平谷区熊儿寨长城
Xiong'erzhai Great Wall, Pinggu District, Beijing

河北省滦平县金山岭砖垛子楼长城
Zhuanduozi Pass Section Jinshanling Great Wall, Luanping County, Hebei Province

河北省滦平县金山岭长城
Jinshanling Great Wall, Luanping County, Hebei Province

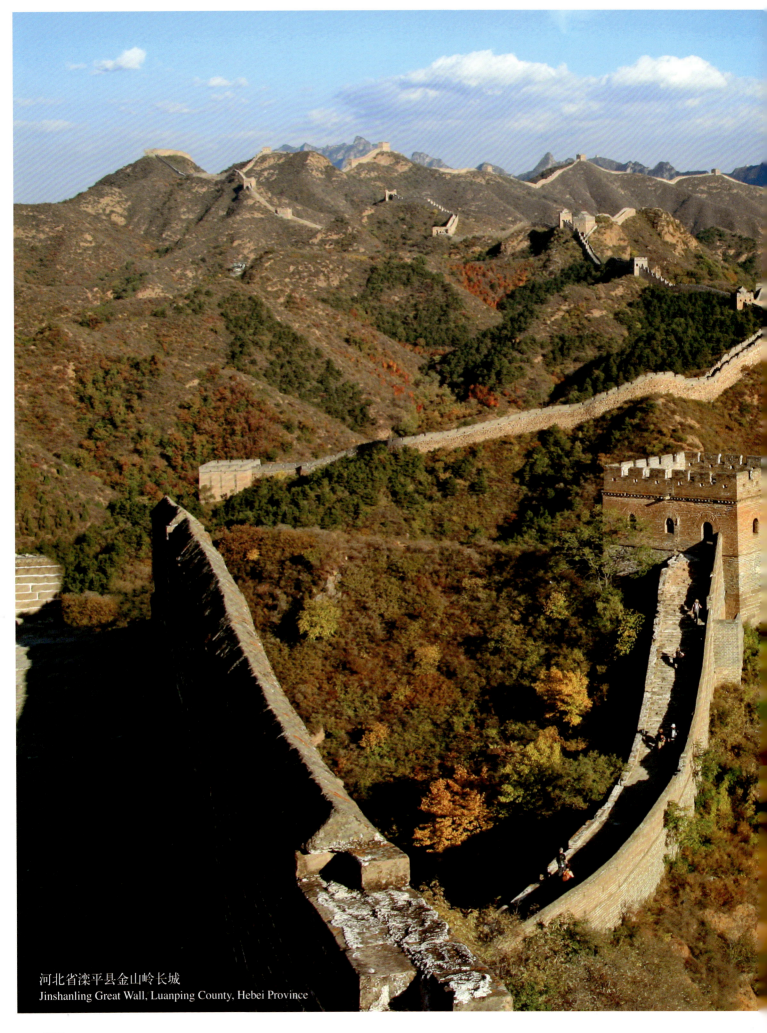

河北省滦平县金山岭长城
Jinshanling Great Wall, Luanping County, Hebei Province

河北省滦平县金山岭长城障墙
Blocking Walls of Jinshanling Great Wall, Luanping County, Hebei Province

河北省滦平县金山岭长城
Jinshanling Great Wall, Luanping County, Hebei Province

河北省滦平县金山岭长城
Jinshanling Great Wall, Luanping County, Hebei Province

河北省滦平县金山岭长城与北京市密云县蟠龙山长城交界处
The Junction Jinshanling Great Wall in Luanping County, Hebei Province and Panlongshan Great Wall in Miyun County, Beijing

北京市密云县蟠龙山长城
Panlongshan Great Wall, Miyun County, Beijing

北京市密云县司马台长城
Simatai Great Wall, Miyun County, Beijing

北京市密云县司马台长城
Simatai Great Wall, Miyun County, Beijing

北京市密云县石城镇长城
Shichengzhen Great Wall, Miyun County, Beijing

北京市怀柔区大水峪村青龙峡长城
Qinglongxia Great Wall at Dashuiyu Village, Huairou District, Beijing

北京市怀柔区官地村长城
Guandicun Great Wall, Huairou District, Beijing

北京市怀柔区慕田峪村长城
Mutianyu Great Wall, Huairou District, Beijing.

北京市怀柔区慕田峪村长城
Mutianyu Great Wall, Huairou District, Beijing.

北京市怀柔区西栅子村长城
Xizhazicun Great Wall, Huairou District, Beijing

北京市怀柔区西栅子村长城
Xizhazicun Great Wall, Huairou District, Beijing

北京市怀柔区西栅子村长城
Xizhazicun Great Wall, Huairou District, Beijing

北京市怀柔区西栅子村长城
Xizhazicun Great Wall, Huairou District, Beijing

北京市怀柔区大榛峪村五队东长城
Eastern Great Wall in 5th Production Team, Dazhenyu Village, Huairou District, Beijing

北京市怀柔区大榛峪村响水湖西段长城
Western Section of Xiangsi Lake Great Wall at Dazhenyu Village, Huairou District, Beijing

北京市怀柔区大榛峪村响水湖西段长城
Western Section of Xiangshui Lake Great Wall at Dazhenyu Village, Huairou District, Beijing

北京市怀柔区三岔村南水关东段长城
Eastern Section of Nanshuiguan Great Wall at Sancha Village, Huairou District, Beijing

北京市怀柔区东宫村长城
Donggongcun Great Wall, Huairou District, Beijing

北京市怀柔区东宫村长城
Donggongcun Great Wall, Huairou District, Beijing

北京市怀柔区黄花城村长城
Huanghuacheng Great Wall, Huairou District, Beijing

1~4. 北京市怀柔区黄花城村长城
Huanghuacheng Great Wall, Huairou District, Beijing

北京市怀柔区黄花城村长城
Huanghuacheng Great Wall, Huairou
District, Beijing

北京市怀柔区西水峪村长城
Xishuiyucun Great Wall, Huairou
District, Beijing

北京市延庆县香屯村长城
Xiangtuncun Great Wall, Yanqing
County, Beijing

北京市延庆县石佛寺村长城
Shifosicun Great Wall, Yanqing County, Beijing

$\dfrac{1}{2}$

1~2.北京市延庆县石佛寺村长城
Shifosicun Great Wall, Yanqing County, Beijing

北京市延庆县岔道村长城
Chadaocun Great Wall, Yanqing County, Beijing

北京市延庆县岔道村长城
Chadaocun Great Wall, Yanqing County, Beijing

北京市延庆县岔道村长城
Chagaoeun Great Wall, Yanqing County, Beijing

北京市延庆县东沟村长城
Donggoueun Great Wall, Yanqing County, Beijing

北京市延庆县石峡村长城
Shixiacun Great Wall, Yanqing County, Beijing

北京市延庆县石峡村长城
Shixiacun Great Wall, Yanqing County, Beijing

北京市延庆县石峡村长城
Shixiacun Great Wall, Yanqing County, Beijing

北京市延庆县石峡村长城
Shixiacun Great Wall, Yanqing County, Beijing

北京市延庆县石峡村长城
Shixiacun Great Wall, Yanqing County, Beijing

1 | 2

1.北京市延庆县石峡村长城
Shixiacun Great Wall, Yanqing County, Beijing

2.北京市延庆县石峡村长城
Shixiacun Great Wall, Yanqing County, Beijing

1～3.北京市昌平区长峪城长城
Changyucheng Great Wall, Changping District, Beijing

北京市昌平区长峪城长城
Changyucheng Great Wall, Changping District, Beijing

北京市昌平区长峪城长城
Changyucheng Great Wall, Changping District, Beijing

北京市昌平区长峪城长城
Changyucheng Great Wall, Changping District, Beijing

河北省怀来县庙港样边长城
Miaogangyangbian Great Wall, Huailai County, Hebei Province

河北省涞水县蔡树庵长城
Caishu'an Great Wall, Laishui County, Hebei Province

河北省涞源县乌龙沟长城
Wulonggou Great Wall, Laiyuan County, Hebei Province

河北省阜平县长城岭口长城
Changchenglingkou Great Wall, Fuping County, Hebei Province

河北省涞源县浮图峪长城
Futuyu Great Wall, Laiyuan County, Hebei Province

河北省涞源县白石口长城
Baishikou Great Wall, Laiyuan County, Hebei Province

河北省涞源县白石口长城
Baishikou Great Wall, Laiyuan County, Hebei Province

河北省涞源县湖海口长城
Huhaikou Great Wall, Laiyuan County, Hebei Province

河北省赤城县三棵树长城
Sankeshu Great Wall, Chicheng County, Hebei Province

河北省赤城县三棵树长城
Sankeshu Great Wall, Chicheng County, Hebei Province

河北省张家口市桥西区长城
Great Wall in Qiaoxi District, Zhangjiakou City, Hebei Province

河北省张家口市桥西区长城
Great Wall in Qiaoxi District, Zhangjiakou City, Hebei Province

河北省淮安县赵家窑长城
Zhaojiayao Great Wall, Huai'an County, Hebei Province

山西省天镇县十六墩长城
Shiliudun Great Wall, Tianzhen County,
Shanxi Province

内蒙古自治区
兴和县头道边村长城
Toudaobian Great Wall, Xinghe
County, Inner Mongolia Autonomous
Region

山西省天镇县保平堡长城
Baopingbu Great Wall, Tianzhen County,
Shanxi Province

山西省天镇县薛三墩长城
Xuesandun Great Wall, Tianzhen County, Shanxi Province

山西省天镇县袁治梁长城
Yuanzhiliang Great Wall, Tianzhen County, Shanxi Province

1
―
2

内蒙古自治区清水河县楝木塔长城
Shumuta Great Wall, Qingshuihe County, Inner
Mongolia Autonomous Region

内蒙古自治区清水河县正泥土塲长城
Zhengnituyan Great Wall, Qingshuihe County, Inner
Mongolia Autonomous Region

内蒙古自治区清水河县阎王鼻子长城
Yanwangbizi Great Wall, Qingshuihe County, Inner Mongolia Autonomous Region

山西省偏关县北场长城
Beichang Great Wall, Pianguan County, Shanxi Province

山西省山阴县新广武长城
Xinguangwu Great Wall,
Shanyin County, Shanxi
Province

山西省山阴县新广武长城
Xinguangwu Great Wall,
Shanyin County, Shanxi
Province

山西省繁峙县竹帛口长城
Zhubokou Great Wall, Fanzhi
County, Shanxi Province

山西省神池县南寨长城
Nanzhai Great Wall, Shenchi County, Shanxi Province

山西省代县白草口长城
Baicaokou Great Wall, Daixian County, Shanxi Province

1		
2	3	4

1.陕西省神木县水头沟山险
Shuitougou Steep Mountain Wall, Shenmu County, Shaanxi Province

2.陕西省神木县泥河村长城
 Nihecun Great Wall, Shenmu County, Shaanxi Province

3.陕西省神木县大柏油堡长城
Dabaiyoubu Great Wall, Shenmu County, Shaanxi Province

4.陕西省神木县大柏堡村长城
Dabaibucun Great Wall, Shenmu County, Shaanxi Province

$$\frac{1}{2}$$

1.陕西省神木县奥庄则长城

Aozhuangze Great Wall, Shenmu County, Shaanxi Province

2.陕西省神木县草湾沟村长城

Caowangoucun Great Wall, Shenmu County, Shaanxi Province

1.陕西省神木县水掌村长城
Shuizhangcun Great Wall, Shenmu County, Shaanxi Province

2.陕西省榆林市榆阳区常乐堡长城
Changlebu Great Wall in Yuyang District, Yulin City, Shaanxi Province

$\dfrac{1}{2}$

1.陕西省榆林市榆阳区镇北台长城
Zhenbeitai Great Wall in Yuyang District,
Yulin City, Shaanxi Province

2.陕西省榆林市榆阳区谷地峁村长城
Gudimaocun Great Wall in Yuyang
District, Yulin City, Shaanxi Province

陕西省定边县三楼村长城
Sanloucun Great Wall, Dingbian County, Shaanxi Province

陕西省定边县王圈梁村长城
Wangquanliangcun Great Wall, Dingbian County, Shaanxi Province

内蒙古自治区鄂托克前旗长城大边与二边
The Primary Wall and Secondary Wall of the
Great Wall at Otog Front Banner, Inner Mongolia
Autonomous Region

内蒙古自治区鄂尔多斯
市特布德长城女墙与藏
身坑
The Parapet and Foxholes
on the Great Wall at Tebude,
Ordos City, Inner Mongolia
Autonomous Region

宁夏回族自治区灵武市横城村长城
Hengchengcun Great Wall, Lingwu City,
Ningxia Hui Autonomous Region

内蒙古自治区阿拉善左旗赤木口长城
Chimukou Great Wall, Alxa Left Banner, Inner Mongolia Autonomous Region

内蒙古自治区阿拉善左旗赤木口长城
Chimukou Great Wall, Alxa Left Banner, Inner Mongolia Autonomous Region

内蒙古自治区阿拉善左旗赤木口长城
Chimukou Great Wall, Alxa Left Banner, Inner Mongolia Autonomous Region

内蒙古自治区阿拉善左旗磨石口长城
Moshikou Great Wall, Alxa Left Banner, Inner Mongolia Autonomous Region

内蒙古自治区阿拉善左旗北岔口长城
Beichakou Great Wall, Alxa Left Banner, Inner Mongolia Autonomous Region

内蒙古自治区阿拉善左旗北岔口长城
Beichakou Great Wall, Alxa Left Banner, Inner Mongolia Autonomous Region

<table>
<tr><td>1</td><td>2</td></tr>
<tr><td colspan="2">3</td></tr>
</table>

1.内蒙古自治区阿拉善左旗北岔口长城二边
Secondary Wall (erbian) of Beichakou Great Wall, Alxa Left Banner, Inner Mongolia Autonomous Region

2～3.内蒙古自治区阿拉善左旗柳木高长城
Liumugao Great Wall, Alxa Left Banner, Inner Mongolia Autonomous Region

宁夏回族自治区青铜峡市北岔口西长城
Western Section of Beichakou Great Wall, Qingtongxia City, Ningxia Hui Autonomous Region

宁夏回族自治区青铜峡市北岔口长城与壕堑（西长城）
Western Section of Beichakou Great Wall and Auxiliary Trenches, Qingtongxia City, Ningxia Hui Autonomous Region

宁夏回族自治区石嘴山市大武口区归德沟西长城
Western Great Wall, Guidegou, Dawukou District, Shizuishan City, Ningxia Hui Autonomous Region

1	2
3	

1.宁夏回族自治区永宁县三关口以南西长城
Western Great Wall to the south of Sanguankou, Yongning County, Ningxia Hui Autonomous Region

2.宁夏回族自治区中卫市沙坡头区上河沿西长城
Western Great Wall, Shangheyan, Shapotou District, Zhongwei City, Ningxia Hui Autonomous Region

3.宁夏回族自治区中卫市沙坡头区上滩苇子坑西长城
Western Great Wall, Shangtan Weizikeng, Shapotou District, Zhongwei City, Ningxia Hui Autonomous Region

1
—
2
—
3

1.甘肃省靖远县长城黄家洼山壕堑
Huangjiawa Hill Trenches, Jingyuan County, Gansu Province

2.甘肃省靖远县小口村"封沟墙"（内侧）
Xiaokou Village "Ditch Blocking Wall", Jingyuan County, Gansu Province (Inner Side)

3.甘肃省靖远县小口村"封沟墙"（外侧）
Xiaokou Village "Ditch Blocking Wall", Jingyuan County, Gansu Province (Outer Side)

甘肃省景泰县麦窝长城
Maiwo Great Wall, Jingtai County, Gansu Province

甘肃省永登县荒滩长城
Huangtan Great Wall, Yongdeng County, Gansu Province

$$\frac{1}{2 \quad 3 \quad 4 \quad 5}$$

1.甘肃省天祝藏族自治县石洞沟梁长城
Shidonggouliang Great Wall, Tianzhu Tibetan Autonomous County, Gansu Province

2.甘肃省天祝藏族自治县石洞沟梁长城及乌鞘岭长城远景
Distant Views of Shidonggouliang Great Wall and Wushaoaoling Great Wall, Tianzhu Tibetan Autonomous County, Gansu Province

3.甘肃省古浪县七墩台长城
Qiduntai Great Wall in Gulang County, Gansu Province

4.甘肃省古浪县马场长城
Machang (Horse Ranch) Great Wall in Gulang County, Gansu Province

5.甘肃省古浪县光辉长城
Guanghui Great Wall in Gulang County, Gansu Province

甘肃省古浪县光辉长城
Guanghui Great Wall in Gulang County, Gansu Province

甘肃省古浪其圆墩长城
Yuandun Great Wall in Gulang County, Gansu Province

1
—
2 3

1~2.甘肃省武威市凉州区土塔长城
Tuta Great Wall, Liangzhou District,
Wuwei City, Gansu Province

3.甘肃省武威市凉州区五墩长城
Wudun Great Wall, Liangzhou District,
Wuwei City, Gansu Province

甘肃省永昌县方沟农场长城
Fanggou Farm Great Wall, Yongchang County, Gansu Province

甘肃省永昌县华家沟农场长城
Huajiagou Farm Great Wall, Yongchang County, Gansu Province

甘肃省永昌县华家沟农场长城
Huajiagou Farm Great Wall, Yongchang County, Gansu Province

甘肃省永昌县青山堡长城
Qingshanbu Great Wall, Yongchang County, Gansu Province

甘肃省永昌县毛卜喇长城
Maopula Great Wall, Yongchang County, Gansu Province

甘肃省永昌县毛卜喇长城
Maopula Great Wall, Yongchang County, Gansu Province

```
  1
------
 2   3
```

1.甘肃省永昌县水泉子壕堑
Shuiquanzi Trenches, Yongchang County, Gansu Province

2.甘肃省山丹县羊虎沟长城
Yanghugou Great Wall, Shandan County, Gansu Province

3.甘肃省山丹县峡口长城
Xiakou Great Wall, Shandan County, Gansu Province

1
—
2   3

1.甘肃省山丹县峡口长城
Xiakou Great Wall, Shandan County, Gansu Province

2.甘肃省山丹县新河长城
Xinhe Great Wall, Shandan County, Gansu Province

3.甘肃省山丹县新河长城（墙体、壕堑并行）
Xinhe Great Wall, Shandan County, Gansu Province (walls and trenches in parallel)

甘肃省山丹县三十里堡长城
Sanshilibu Great Wall, Shandan County, Gansu Province

甘肃省山丹县三十里堡长城
Sanshilibu Great Wall, Shandan County, Gansu Province

甘肃省张掖市甘州区鸳鸯池壕堑
Yuanyangchi Trenches, Ganzhou District, Zhangye City, Gansu Province

甘肃省酒泉市肃州区边湾滩长城
Bianwantan Great Wall, Suzhou District, Jiuquan City, Gansu Province

甘肃省嘉峪关市三墩长城
Sandun Great Wall, Jiayuguan City, Gansu Province

甘肃省嘉峪关市三墩壕堑
Sandun Trenches, Jiayuguan City, Gansu Province

甘肃省嘉峪关市暗壁壕堑及长城
The Walled Trenches and Great Wall in
Jiayuguan City, Gansu Province

青海省乐都县石家沟壕堑
Shijiagou Trenches, Ledu County, Qinghai
Province

青海省互助县泥麻村长城
Nimacun Great Wall, Huzhu County, Qinghai Province

青海省互助县马家庄长城墙体与内侧壕堑
Majiazhuang Great Wall and interior trenches, Huzhu County, Qinghai Province

青海省大通县下庙沟长城
Xiamiaogou Great Wall, Datong County, Qinghai Province

青海省湟中县新城长城
Xincheng Great Wall, Huangzhong County, Qinghai Province

明 长 城 THE MING GREAT WALL

敌台、马面
Watchtowers and Bastions

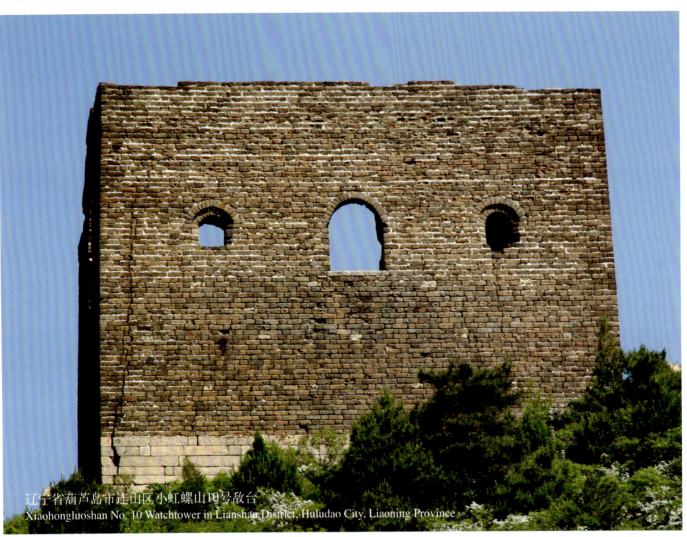

辽宁省葫芦岛市连山区小虹螺山10号敌台
Xiaohongluoshan No. 10 Watchtower in Lianshan District, Huludao City, Liaoning Province

辽宁省绥中县鼓山2号敌台
Gushan No.2 Watchtower in Suizhong County, Liaoning Province

1.辽宁省绥中县蔓枝草2号敌台

Wanzhicao No.2 Watchtower in Suizhong County, Liaoning Province

2~3.辽宁省绥中县蔓枝草3号敌台

Wanzhicao No.3 Watchtower in Suizhong County, Liaoning Province

辽宁省绥中县蔓枝草3号敌台
Wanzhicao No.3 Watchtower in Suizhong County, Liaoning Province

辽宁省绥中县锥子山2号敌台
Zhuizishan No.2 Watchtower in Suizhong County, Liaoning Province

河北省抚宁县九门口关城子母台
Zimutai Beacon Tower of Jiumenkou Pass in Funing County,
Hebei Province

1.河北省抚宁县292号敌台
No. 292 Watchtower in Funing County, Hebei Province

2.河北省抚宁县董家口村8号敌台
Dongjiakou No. 8 Watchtower in Funing County, Hebei Province

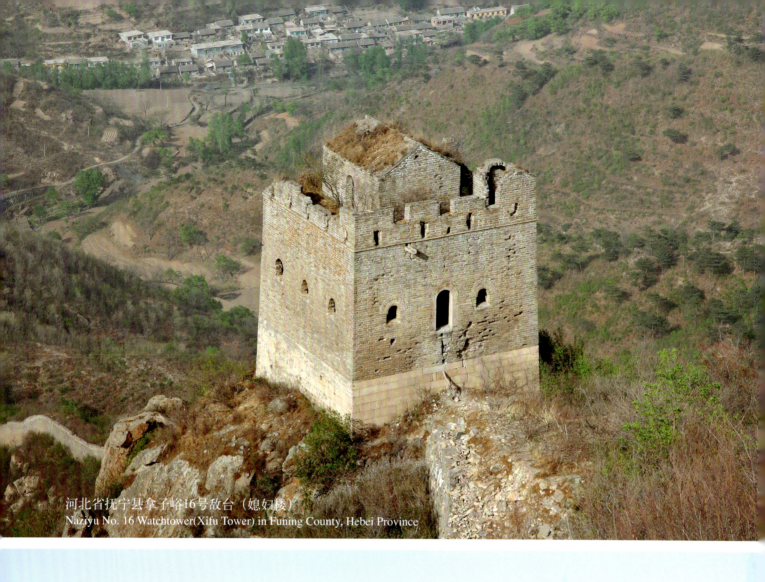

河北省抚宁县拿子峪16号敌台（媳妇楼）
Naziyu No. 16 Watchtower(Xifu Tower) in Funing County, Hebei Province

河北省抚宁县花场峪13号敌台
Huachangyu No. 13 Watchtower in Funing County, Hebei Province

河北省卢龙县刘家口关水关墩
Shuiguandun Watchtower in Liujiakou Pass, Lulong county, Hebei Province

河北省迁安市94号敌台
No. 94 Watchtower in Qian'an City, Hebei Province

河北省迁安市2号敌台
No. 2 Watchtower in Qian'an City, Hebei Province

河北省迁安市63号敌台
No. 63 Watchtower in Qian'an City, Hebei Province

河北省迁安市白羊峪神威楼
Shenwei Tower of Baiyangyu Great Wall, Qian'an City, Hebei Province

河北省迁安市88号敌台
No. 88 Watchtower in Qian'an City, Hebei Province

1	2
3	4
5	6

1.河北省迁西县头道岭西山7号敌台
Toudaoling Xishan No. 7 Watchtower in Qianxi County, Hebei Province

2.河北省迁西县榆木岭1号敌台
Yumuling No. 1 Watchtower in Qianxi County, Hebei Province

3.河北省迁西县八面峰2号敌台
Bamianfeng No. 2 Watchtower in Qianxi County, Hebei Province

4.河北省迁西县闸扣1号敌台
Zhakou No.1 Watchtower in Qianxi County, Hebei Province

5.河北省迁西县贾庄子1号敌台
Jiazhuangzi No.1 Watchtower in Qianxi County, Hebei Province

6.河北省迁西县龙凤沟2号敌台
Longfenggou No.2 Watchtower in Qianxi County, Hebei Province

$$\frac{1}{2 \ 3 \ 4}$$

1.河北省迁西县潘家口23号敌台
Panjiakou No. 23 Watchtower in Qianxi County, Hebei Province

2.河北省迁西县东城峪1号敌台
Dongchengyu No. 1 Watchtower in Qianxi County, Hebei Province

3.河北省迁西县小河口6号敌台
Xiaohekou No. 6 Watchtower in Qianxi County, Hebei Province

4.河北省遵化市43号敌台
No. 43 Watchtower in Zunhua City, Hebei Province

天津市蓟县赤霞峪7号敌台
Chixiayu No. 7 Watchtower in Jixian County, Tianjin

天津市蓟县青山岭2号敌台
Qingshanling No. 2 Watchtower in Jixian County, Tianjin

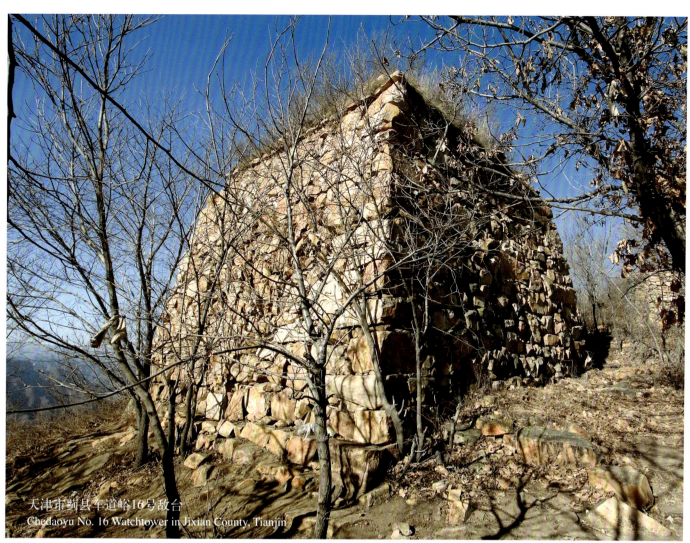

天津市蓟县车道峪16号敌台
Chedaoyu No. 16 Watchtower in Jixian County, Tianjin

天津市蓟县黄崖关3号敌台
No. 3 Watchtower of Huangyaguan Pass, Jixian County, Tianjin

天津市蓟县黄崖关5号敌台
No. 5 Watchtower of Huangyaguan Pass, Jixian County, Tianjin

天津市蓟县黄崖关8号敌台
No. 8 Watchtower of Huangyaguan Pass, Jixian County, Tianjin

天津市蓟县黄崖关20号敌台
No. 20 Watchtower of Huangyaguan Pass, Jixian County, Tianjin

天津市蓟县前干涧1号敌台首层内部
The internal of the first floor of Qianganjian No. 1 Watchtower in Jixian County, Tianjin

北京市平谷区上营城堡敌台
Watchtower of Shangying Fort, Pinggu District, Beijing

北京市密云县新城子镇35号敌台
No. 35 Watchtower in Xinchengzi Township, Miyun County, Beijing

北京市密云县新城子镇51号敌台
No. 51 Watchtower in Xinchengzi Township, Miyun County, Beijing

1 2
―――
3

1.北京市密云县新城子镇67号敌台
No. 67 Watchtower in Xinchengzi Township, Miyun County, Beijing

2.北京市密云县司马台8号敌台
Simatai No. 8 Watchtower in Miyun County, Beijing

3.北京市密云县古北口43号敌台
Gubeikou No. 43 Watchtower in Miyun County, Beijing

1.北京市密云县石城镇17号敌台
No. 17 Watchtower in Shicheng Township,
Miyun County, Beijing

2.北京市密云县石城镇38号敌台
No. 38 Watchtower in Shicheng Township,
Miyun County, Beijing

3.北京市密云县石城镇42号敌台
No. 42 Watchtower in Shicheng Township,
Miyun County, Beijing

1	2
3	

1.北京市怀柔区河防口36号敌台
Hefangkou No. 36 Watchtower in Huairou District, Beijing

2.北京市怀柔区官地村58号敌台
Guandi No. 58 Watchtower in Huairou District, Beijing

3.北京市怀柔区官地村59号敌台
Guandi No. 59 Watchtower in Huairou District, Beijing

$$\frac{1}{2 \quad 3}$$
$$4$$

1.北京市怀柔区长园村67号敌台
 Changyuan No. 67 Watchtower in Huairou District, Beijing

2.北京市怀柔区莲花池村70号敌台
Lianhuachi No. 70 Watchtower in Huairou District, Beijing

3.北京市怀柔区莲花池村71号敌台
Lianhuachi No. 71 Watchtower in Huairou District, Beijing

4.北京市怀柔区莲花池村72号敌台
Lianhuachi No. 72 Watchtower in Huairou District, Beijing

北京市怀柔区莲花池村镇关台
Zhenguantai (Watchtower) of Lianhuachi Great Wall, Huairou District, Beijing

北京市怀柔区莲花池村84号敌台（大角楼）
Lianhuachi No. 84 Watchtower (Dajiao Tower) in Huairou District, Beijing

北京市怀柔区莲花池村84号敌台（大角楼）
Lianhuachi No. 84 Watchtower (Dajiao Tower) in Huairou District, Beijing

北京市怀柔区大榛峪村五队东墙体177号敌台
Eastern Wall, 5th Production Team No. 177 Watchtower in Dazhenyu Village, Huairou District, Beijing

北京市怀柔区大榛峪村五队东墙体179号敌台
Eastern Wall, 5th Production Team No. 179 Watchtower in Dazhenyu Village, Huairou District, Beijing

北京市怀柔区大榛峪村180号敌台（五眼楼）
Wuyanlou No. 180 (Watch tower), in Dazhenyu Village, Huairou District, Beijing

北京市昌平区高楼5号敌台
Gaolou No. 5 Watchtower, Changping District, Beijing

北京市昌平区高楼8号敌台
Gaolou No. 8 Watchtower, Changping District, Beijing

北京市昌平区高楼14号敌台
Gaolou No. 14 Watchtower,
Changping District, Beijing

北京市昌平区高楼14号敌台内部
The internal of Gaolou No. 14
Watchtower, Changping District,
Beijing

北京市昌平区高楼15号敌台
Gaolou No. 15 Watchtower,
Changping District, Beijing

北京市门头沟区沿河口村3号敌台
Yanhekou No. 3 Watchtower in Mentougou District, Beijing

北京市门头沟区
沿河口村4号敌台
Yanhekou No. 4 Watchtower in
Mentougou District, Beijing

北京市门头沟区沿河口村5号敌台
Yanhekou No. 5 Watchtower in Mentougou District, Beijing

北京市门头沟区龙门口村沿字10号敌台
No. 10 Watchtower of "Yan" Series in Longmenkou Village, Mentougou District, Beijing

北京市门头沟区龙门口村沿字11号敌台
No. 11 Watchtower of "Yan" Series at Longmenkou Village, Mentougou District, Beijing

河北省涞水县蔡树庵村1号马面
Caishu'an No. 1 Bastion in Laishui County, Hebei Province

河北省涞源县乌龙沟10号敌台
Wulonggou No. 10 Watchtower in Laiyuan
County, Hebei Province

河北省涞源县南芦台村20号敌台
Nanlutai No. 20 Watchtower in Laiyuan County, Hebei Province

河北省涞源县湖海村12号敌台
Huhai No. 12 Watchtower in Laiyuan County, Hebei Province

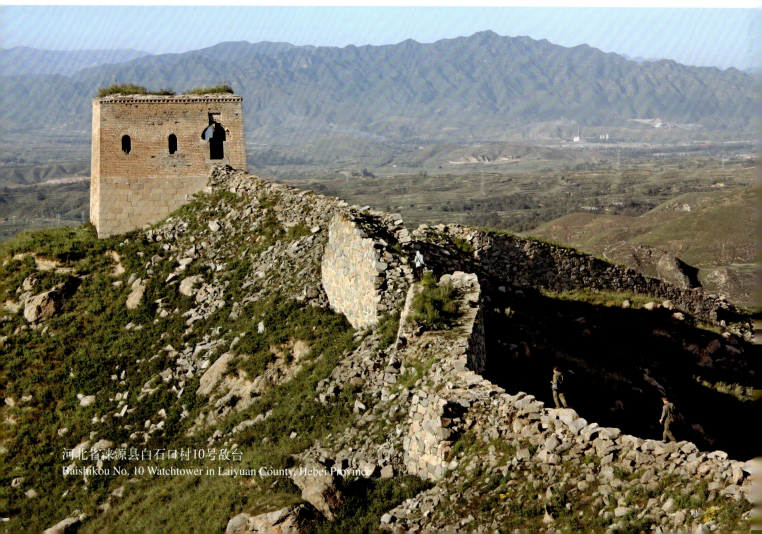

河北省涞源县白石口村10号敌台
Baishikou No. 10 Watchtower in Laiyuan County, Hebei Province

河北省涞源县石窝村7号敌台
Shiwo No. 7 Watchtower in Laiyuan County, Hebei Province

河北省涞源县插箭岭5号敌台
Chajianling No. 5 Watchtower in Laiyuan County, Hebei Province

1	2
3	4
5	

1.河北省赤城县万水泉6号敌台
Wanshuiquan No. 6 Watchtower in Chicheng
County, Hebei Province

2.河北省赤城县平路口敌台
Pinglukou Watchtower in Chicheng County,
Hebei Province

3.河北省赤城县庄科1号敌台
Zhuangke No. 1 Watchtower in Chicheng County, Hebei Province

4.河北省赤城县小庄科2号敌台（盘道界楼）
Xiaozhuangke No. 2 Watchtower(Pandaojie Tower) in Chicheng County,
Hebei Province

5.河北省赤城县马莲口4号敌台
Maliankou No. 4 Watchtower in Chicheng County, Hebei Province

1	2
3	4

1.山西省左云县镇宁楼
Zhenning Tower in Zuoyun County, Shanxi Province

2.山西省偏关县寺沟10号敌台
Sigou No. 10 Watchtower in Pianguan County, Shanxi Province

3.山西省繁峙县茨沟营茨字21号敌台
No. 21 Watchtower of "Ci" Series in Cigouying Village, Fanshi County, Shanxi Province

4.山西省灵丘县牛邦口茨字37号敌台
No. 37 Watchtower of "Ci" Series in Niubangkou Village, Lingqiu County, Shanxi Province

	1	
2		3
	4	

1.内蒙古自治区兴和县头道边村1号敌台
Toudaobian No. 1 Watchtower in Xinghe County, Inner Mongolia Autonomous Region

2.内蒙古自治区丰镇县隆盛庄敌台
Longshengzhuang Watchtower in Fengzhen County, Inner Mongolia Autonomous Region

3.内蒙古自治区丰镇县隆盛庄敌台内部
The Internal of the Longshengzhuang Watchtower in Fengzhen County, Inner Mongolia Autonomous Region

4.内蒙古自治区凉城县东沟敌台
Donggou Watchtower in Liangcheng County, Inner Mongolia Autonomous Region

1	2
3	
4	5

1.内蒙古自治区和林格尔县上红台1号敌台
Shanghongtai No. 1 Watchtower in Horinger County, Inner Mongolia Autonomous Region

2.内蒙古自治区清水河县板申沟1号敌台
Banshengou No. 1 Watchtower in Qingshuihe County, Inner Mongolia Autonomous Region

3.内蒙古自治区清水河县八墩3号敌台
Badun No. 3 Watchtower in Qingshuihe County, Inner Mongolia Autonomous Region

4.内蒙古自治区清水河县小元峁1号敌台
Xiaoyuanmao No. 1 Watchtower in Qingshuihe County, Inner Mongolia Autonomous Region

5.内蒙古自治区准格尔旗竹里台敌台　Zhulitai Watchtower in Jungar Banner, Inner Mongolia Autonomous Region

陕西省府谷县凤凰塔村长城马面
Brick-lined Bastion (Mamian) in Fenghuangta Village, Shenmu County, Shaanxi Province

陕西省神木县庄则梁—歇马沟山险分布的敌台
Watchtowers Distributed along the Steep Mountain Wall at Zhuangzeliang through Xiemagou, Shenmu County, Shaanxi Province

1
2 3 4

1～4.陕西省神木县水头沟村敌台及内部结构
Shuitougou Watchtower in Shenmu County, Shaanxi Province and its Internal
Structure

陕西省神木县水头沟村敌台与远处包砖敌台
Shuitougou Watchtower in Shenmu County, Shaanxi Province and the brick-lined Watchtower in the distance

1
———
2 3

1.陕西省神木县石墕子2号敌台
Shihezi No. 2 Watchtower in Shenmu County, Shaanxi Province

2.陕西省神木县山峰则4号敌台
Shanfengze No. 4 Watchtower in Shenmu County, Shaanxi Province

3.陕西省神木县水掌村包砖马面
Shuizhang Brick-lined Bastion (Mamian) in Shenmu County, Shaanxi Province

陕西省榆林市榆阳区镇北台敌台
Zhenbeitai Watchtower in Yuyang District, Yulin City, Shaanxi Province

陕西省榆林市榆阳区镇北台敌台全景
Panoramic View of the Zhenbeitai Watchtower in Yuyang District, Yulin City, Shaanxi Province

$$\frac{1}{2}$$

1.陕西省横山县芦沟村边墙梁敌台
Bianqiangliang Watchtower in Lugou Village, Hengshan County, Shaanxi Province

2.陕西省定边县惠楼村7号敌台（五里墩）
Huilou No. 7 Watchtower (Wulidun) in Dingbian County, Shaanxi Province

236

内蒙古自治区鄂托克前旗特布德长城二边10号敌台
Tebude No. 10 Watchtower on the Secondary Wall of the Great Wall in Otog Front Banner, Inner Mongolia Autonomous Region

内蒙古自治区阿拉善左旗北岔口长城二边1号敌台
Beichakou No. 1 Watchtower on the Secondary Wall of the Great Wall in Alxa Left Banner, Inner Mongolia Autonomous Region

甘肃省永登县马家坪敌台
Majiaping Watchtower in Yongdeng
County, Gansu Province

甘肃省古浪县
永丰滩暗门墩1号敌台
Anmendun No.1 Watchtower
in Gulang County, Gansu
Province

甘肃省古浪县圆墩3号敌台
Yuandun No. 3 Watchtower in Gulang County,
Gansu Province

1	2
3	4

1.甘肃省武威市凉州区长丰4号敌台
Changfeng No. 4 Watchtower in Liangzhou District, Wuwei City, Gansu Province

2.甘肃省武威市凉州区五墩1号敌台
Wudun No. 1 Watchtower in Liangzhou District, Wuwei City, Gansu Province

3.甘肃省高台县夹山塘墩
Jiashantang Watchtower, Gaotai County, Gansu Province

4.甘肃省酒泉市肃州区明沙窝1号敌台
Mingshawo No. 1 Watchtower in Suzhou District, Jiuquan City, Gansu Province

甘肃省嘉峪关市野麻湾4号敌台
Yemawan No. 4 Watchtower in Jiayuguan City, Gansu Province

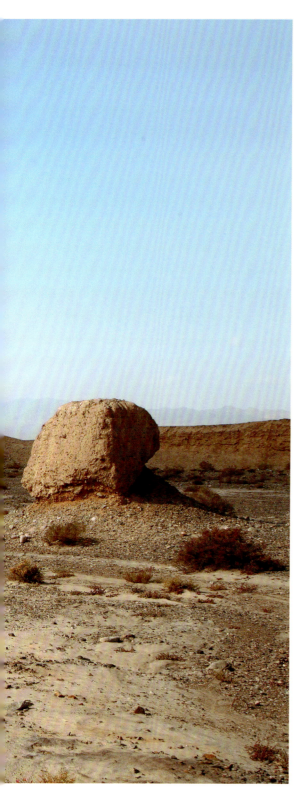

甘肃省嘉峪关市野麻湾10号敌台
Yemawan No. 10 Watchtower in Jiayuguan City, Gansu Province

甘肃省嘉峪关市暗壁3号敌台
Anbi No. 3 Watchtower , Jiayuguan City, Gansu Province

甘肃省嘉峪关二墩
Jiayuguan No. 2 Watchtower, Gansu Province

青海省大通县上庙沟敌台
Shangmiaogou Watchtower in Datong County, Qinghai Province

青海省大通县元树尔敌台
Yuanshu'er Watchtower in Datong County, Qinghai Province

青海省贵德县贵德古城西墙马面
Bastion (Mamian) on the Western Wall of Guide Old Town, Guide County, Qinghai Province

明　长　城　THE MING GREAT WALL

烽火台
Beacon Towers

辽宁省黑山县江台北山烽火台
Beishan Beacon Tower at Jiangtai Village, Heishan County, Liaoning Province

辽宁省黑山县义和屯烽火台
Yihetun Beacon Tower in Heishan County, Liaoning Province

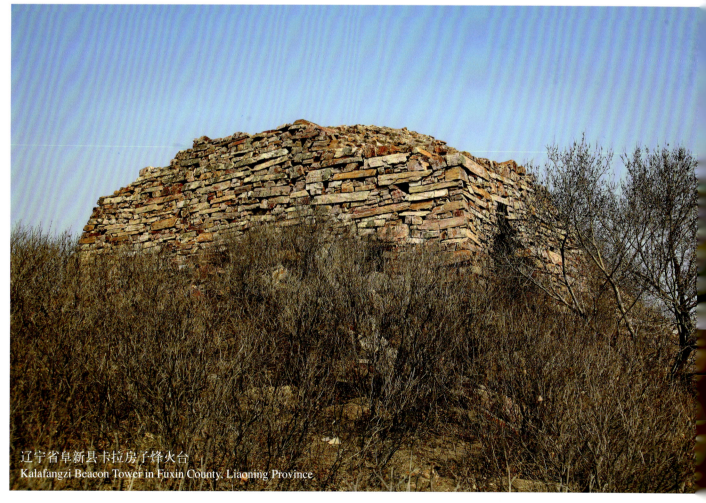

辽宁省阜新县卡拉房子烽火台
Kalafangzi Beacon Tower in Fuxin County, Liaoning Province

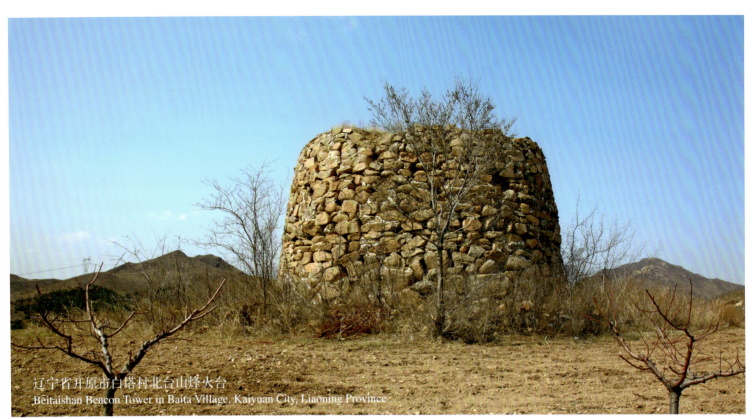

辽宁省开原市白塔村北台山烽火台
Beitaishan Beacon Tower in Baita Village, Kaiyuan City, Liaoning Province

辽宁省绥中县蔓枝草1号烽火台
Wanzhicao No. 1 Beacon Tower in Suizhong County, Liaoning Province

辽宁省绥中县蔓枝草1号烽火台
Wanzhicao No. 1 Beacon Tower in Suizhong County, Liaoning Province

$$\frac{1}{\frac{2}{3}}$$

1.河北省秦皇岛市山海关区2号烽火台
Shanhaiguan No. 2 Beacon Tower in
Qinhuangdao City, Hebei Province

2.河北省青龙县拿子峪8号烽火台
Naziyu No. 8 Beacon Tower in Qinglong
County, Hebei Province

3.河北省卢龙县桃林口5号烽火台
Taolinkou No. 5 Beacon Tower in Lulong
County, Hebei Province

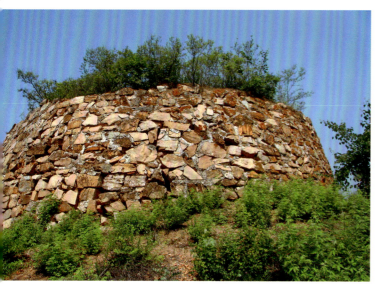

1	2
3	4
5	

1.河北省迁安市河流口9号烽火台
Heliukou No. 9 Beacon Tower in Qian'an City, Hebei Province

2.河北省迁西县大岭寨口北山3号烽火台
Dalingzhaikou Beishan No. 3 Beacon Tower in Qianxi County, Hebei Province

3.河北省迁西县兰城沟1号烽火台
Lanchenggou No. 1 Beacon Tower in Qianxi County, Hebei Province

4.河北省迁西县李家峪2号烽火台
Lijiayu No. 2 Beacon Tower in Qianxi County, Hebei Province

5.河北省宽城县新甸子9号烽火台
Xindianzi No. 9 Beacon Tower in Kuancheng County, Hebei Province

河北省滦平县金山岭2号烽火台
Jinshanling No. 2 Beacon Tower in Luanping County, Hebei Province

河北省赤城县万水泉4号烽火台
Wanshuiquan No. 4 Beacon Tower in Chicheng
County, Hebei Province

河北省赤城县清泉堡永照楼
Yongzhao Tower in Qingquanbu Fortress, Chicheng
County, Hebei Province

河北省赤城县海家窑1号烽火台
Haijiayao No. 1 Beacon Tower in Chicheng
County, Hebei Province

河北省赤城县海家窑7号烽火台
Haijiayao No. 7 Beacon Tower in Chicheng County, Hebei Province

河北省赤城县九棵树2号烽火台
Jiukeshu No. 2 Beacon Tower in Chicheng County, Hebei Province

河北省张家口市桥西区五墩村6号烽火台
Wudun No. 6 Beacon Tower in Qiaoxi
District, Zhangjiakou City, Hebei Province

河北省张家口市桥西区五墩村14号烽火台
Wudun No. 14 Beacon Tower in Qiaoxi
District, Zhangjiakou City, Hebei Province

河北省阳源县起风波2号烽火台
Qifengbo No. 2 Beacon Tower in Yangyuan
County, Hebei Province

1.内蒙古自治区兴和县头道边村1号烽火台

Toudaobian No. 1 Beacon Tower in Xinghe County, Inner Mongolia Autonomous Region

2.内蒙古自治区兴和县头道边村7号烽火台

Toudaobian No. 7 Beacon Tower in Xinghe County, Inner Mongolia Autonomous Region

内蒙古自治区凉城县蓝旗窑1、2号烽火台
Lanqiyao Nos. 1 & 2 Beacon Towers in Liangcheng County, Inner Mongolia Autonomous Region

内蒙古自治区清水河县杨家窑4号烽火台
Yangjiayao No. 4 Beacon Tower in Qingshuihe County, Inner Mongolia Autonomous Region

山西省偏关县川昴上5号烽火台

Chuanangshang No. 5 Beacon Tower in Pianguan County, Shanxi Province

内蒙古自治区清水河县双井子烽火台
Shuangjingzi Beacon Tower in Qingshuihe County, Inner Mongolia Autonomous Region

内蒙古自治区准格尔旗竹里台烽火台
Zhulitai Beacon Tower in Jungar Banner, Inner Mongolia Autonomous Region

山西省河曲县船湾3号烽火台
Chuanwan No. 3 Beacon Tower in Hequ County, Shanxi Province

陕西省府谷县麻二村烽火台
Ma'er Beacon Tower in Fugu County, Shaanxi Province

陕西省神木县板墩墕烽火台
Bandunyan Beacon Tower in Shenmu County, Shaanxi Province

陕西省神木县板墩墕烽火台
Bandunyan Beacon Tower in Shenmu County, Shaanxi Province

宁夏回族自治区盐池县沙坡子
烽火台夯筑围墙
Fence Wall (built of rammed earth)
of Shapozi Beacon Tower in Yanchi
County, Ningxia Hui Autonomous
Region

宁夏回族自治区灵武市东庄子
烽火台
Dongzhuangzi Beacon Tower
in Lingwu City, Ningxia Hui
Autonomous Region

宁夏回族自治区吴忠市利通区
白土岗子烽火台
Baitugangzi Beacon Tower in Litong
District, Wuzhong City, Ningxia Hui
Autonomous Region

内蒙古自治区阿拉善左旗磨石口2号烽火台
Moshikou No. 2 Beacon Tower in Alxa Left Banner, Inner Mongolia Autonomous Region

宁夏回族自治区青铜峡市大柳木皋烽火台
Daliumugao Beacon Tower in Qingtongxia City, Ningxia Hui Autonomous Region

宁夏回族自治区青铜峡市甘城子烽火台
Ganchengzi Beacon Tower in Qingtongxia City, Ningxia Hui Autonomous Region

宁夏回族自治区青铜峡市口子门沟烽火台
Kouzimengou Beacon Tower in Qingtongxia City, Ningxia Hui Autonomous Region

宁夏回族自治区海原县麻春烽火台
Machun Beacon Tower in Haiyuan County, Ningxia Hui Autonomous Region

宁夏回族自治区海原县固原内
边罗山烽火台

Luoshan Beacon Tower of the Guyuan Inner Wall of the Great Wall in
Haiyuan County, Ningxia Hui Autonomous Region

宁夏回族自治区同心县六铺墩烽火台
Liupudun Beacon Tower in Tongxin County, Ningxia Hui Autonomous Region

甘肃省靖远县黄家洼山4号烽火台
Huangjiawashan No. 4 Beacon Tower in Jingyuan County, Gansu Province

甘肃省白银市平川区赵家岘烽火台
Zhaojiaxian Beacon Tower in Pingchuan District, Baiyin City, Gansu Province

甘肃省永登县新站墩
Xinzhan Beacon Tower in Yongdeng County, Gansu Province

甘肃省古浪县青山寺墩
Qingshansi Beacon Tower in Gulang County, Gansu Province

甘肃省古浪县王家墩
Wangjia Beacon Tower in Gulang County, Gansu Province

270

甘肃省武威市凉州区地质六队农场烽火台
The 6th Geological Team Farm Beacon Tower in Liangzhou District, Wuwei City, Gansu Province

甘肃省民勤县河东烽火台
Hedong Beacon Tower in Minqin County, Gansu Province

甘肃省山丹县新河6号烽火台
Xinhe No. 6 Beacon Tower in Shandan County, Gansu Province

甘肃省山丹县西屯2号烽火台
Xitun No. 2 Beacon Tower in Shandan County, Gansu Province

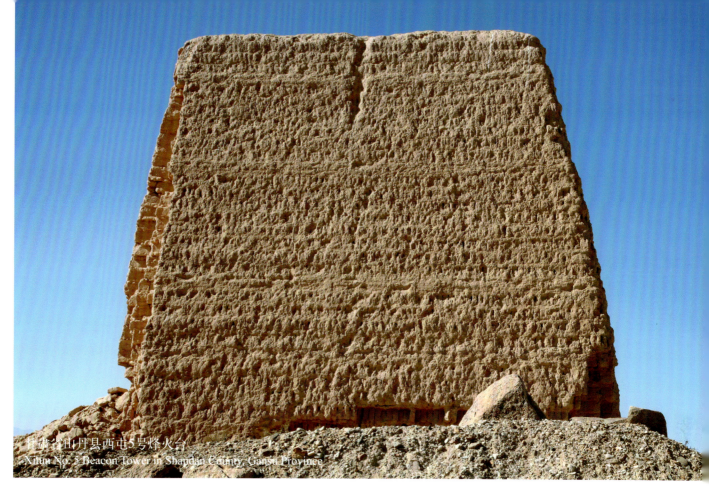

甘肃省山丹县西屯5号烽火台
Xitun No. 5 Beacon Tower in Shandan County, Gansu Province

甘肃省张掖市甘州区红泉8号烽火台
Hongquan No. 8 Beacon Tower in Ganzhou District, Zhangye City, Gansu Province

甘肃省临泽县炭山口墩
Tanshankou Beacon Tower in Linze County, Gansu Province

甘肃省高台县月牙墩
Yueya (Crescent) Beacon Tower in Gaotai County, Gansu Province

甘肃省金塔县梧桐大墩
Wutongdadun Beacon Tower in Jinta County, Gansu Province

甘肃省嘉峪关市一墩（讨赖河墩）
No. 1 Beacon Tower in Jiayuguan City, Gansu Province (Taolaihe Beacon Tower)

青海省乐都县白崖坪村烽火台
Baiyaping Beacon Tower in Ledu County, Qinghai Province

青海省乐都县晁马家村1号烽火台
Chaomajia No. 1 Beacon Tower in Ledu County, Qinghai Province

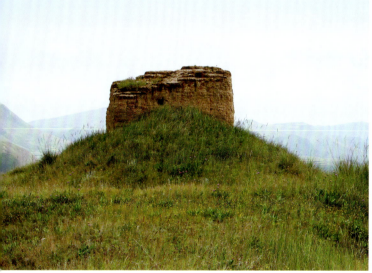

1
___
2　3

1.青海省乐都县仓岭沟3号烽火台远景
Distant view of Canglinggou No. 3 Beacon Tower in Ledu County, Qinghai Province

2.青海省互助县拉卡村1号烽火台
Laka No. 1 Beacon Tower in Huzhu County, Qinghai Province

3.青海省化隆县香里胡拉烽火台
Xianglihula Beacon Tower in Hualong County, Qinghai Province

关、堡

Passes and Fortresses

辽宁省宽甸县赫甸城堡
Hedian Fortress in Kuandian County, Liaoning Province

辽宁省凤城市石城堡
Shichengbu Fortress in Fengcheng City, Liaoning Province

辽宁省北宁市镇边堡
Zhenbianbao Fortress in Beining City, Liaoning Province

辽宁省绥中县永安堡
Yong'anbao Fortress in Suizhong County, Liaoning Province

河北省秦皇岛市山海关区镇东楼（天下第一关）
Zhendong Tower (The First Pass under Heaven), Shanhaiguan District, Qinhuangdao City, Hebei Province

河北省抚宁县箭杆岭关城
Jianganling Pass, Funing County, Hebei Province

河北省抚宁县城子峪关城
Chengziyu Pass, Funing County, Hebei Province

河北省抚宁县石门寨城
Shimenzhai Fortress in Funing County, Hebei Province

河北省迁安市方城
Fangcheng Fortress in Qian'an City, Hebei Province

河北省迁西县青山关关城
Qingshanguan Pass, Qianxi County, Hebei Province

河北省迁西县游乡口谎城
Youxiangkou False Commanding Unit (Huangcheng) in Qianxi County, Hebei Province

河北省遵化市罗文裕东城
Luowenyu Eastern Section of Great Wall Zunhua City, Hebei Province

天津市蓟县古强峪寨堡
Guqiangyu Fortress in Jixian County, Tianjin

天津市蓟县古强峪寨堡东墙
Eastern Wall of the Guqiangyu Fortress in Jixian
County, Tianjin

天津市蓟县青山岭寨堡
Qingshanling Fortress in Jixian County, Tianjin

天津市蓟县黄崖关
Huangyaguan Pass, Jixian County, Tianjin

290

天津市蓟县黄崖关城南门
South Gate of Huangyaguan Pass, Jixian County, Tianjin

天津市蓟县黄崖关城水关
Watergate of Huangyaguan Pass, Jixian County, Tianjin

北京市密云县遥桥峪堡
Yaoqiaoyu Fortress in Miyun County, Beijing

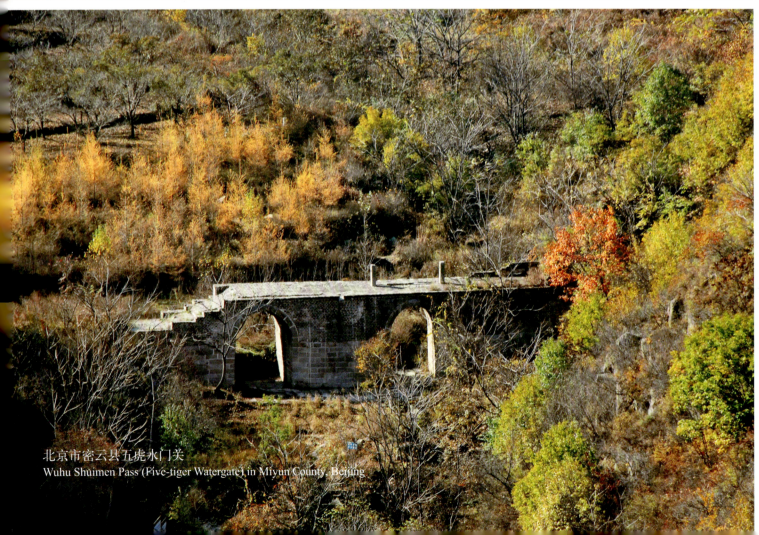

北京市密云县五虎水门关
Wuhu Shuimen Pass (Five-tiger Watergate) in Miyun County, Beijing

北京市密云县黑古关堡
Heiguguan Pass in Miyun County, Beijing

北京市密云县姜毛峪城堡
Jiangmaoyu Fortress in Miyun County, Beijing

河北省赤城县长伸地堡
Changshendi Fortress, Chicheng County,
Hebei Province

河北省赤城县清泉堡
Qingquanbu Fortress in Chicheng County, Hebei Province

河北省赤城县清泉堡东门
Eastern Gate of Qingquanbao Fortress, Chicheng County, Hebei Province

河北省赤城县独石口城堡南墙
Southern Wall of Dushikou Fortress, Chicheng County, Hebei Province

河北省赤城县松树堡北门匾额
Inscription Board on the Northern Gate of Songshubu Fortress, Chicheng County, Hebei Province

河北省赤城县大岭堡东门匾额
Inscription Board on the Eastern Gate of Dalingbu Fortress, Chicheng County, Hebei Province

河北省赤城县城西城门门簪
Gate Peg on the Western Gate of Chicheng County, Hebei Province

河北省张家口市桥西区大境门
Dajing Gate in Qiaoxi District, Zhangjiakou City, Hebei Province

河北省宣化区宣府镇城清远楼
Qingyuan Tower of Xuanfu Command Garrison in Xuanhua District, Zhangjiakou City, Hebei Province

河北省宣化区宣府镇城镇朔楼
Zhenshuo Tower of Xuanfu Command Garrison in Xuanhua District, Zhangjiakou City, Hebei Province

河北省涞水县大龙门堡东门
Eastern Gate of Dalongmenbao Fortress in Laishui County, Hebei Province

河北省易县紫荆关关城
Zijingguan Pass, Yixian County, Hebei Province

河北省易县紫荆关北瓮城东门
The Eastern Gate of the North Barbican of Zijingguan Pass, Yixian County, Hebei Province

河北省涞水具大龙门堡
Dalongmenbao Fortress in Laishui County, Hebei Province

河北省涞源具白石口南门
The Southern Gate of Baishikou Pass in Laiyuan County, Hebei Province

河北省唐县倒马关关城
Daomaguan Pass, Tangxian County, Hebei Province

河北省涞源县狼牙口关
Langyakou Pass, Laiyuan County, Hebei Province

河北省阜平县龙泉关北门
North Gate of Longquan Pass, Fuping County, Hebei Province

河北省井陉县岸底村关口
Andi Pass in Jingxing County, Hebei Province

河北省内丘县鹤度岭关
Heduling Pass in Neiqiu County, Hebei Province

河北省邢台县马岭关关门
Gate of Maling Pass in Xingtai County, Hebei Province

河北省邢台县黄峪榆岭关门
Gate of Huangyuling Pass in Xingtai County, Hebei Province

河北省沙河市支锅岭口关门
Gate of Zhiguolingkou Pass in Shahe City, Hebei Province

山西省代县雁门关
Yanmenguan Pass in Daixian County, Shanxi Province

山西省繁峙县平型关
Pingxingguan Pass in Fanshi County, Shanxi Province

山西省大同市得胜堡内玉皇阁
The Yuhuangge (Jade Emperor Pavilion) in Deshengbao Fortress in Datong City, Shanxi Province

山西省右玉县移民新村大堡
Yiminxincun Fortress in Youyu County, Shanxi Province

山西省右玉县云石堡
Yunshibu Fortress in Youyu County, Shanxi Province

内蒙古自治区和林格尔县黄草梁堡
Huangcaoliang Fortress in Horinger County, Inner Mongolia Autonomous Region

内蒙古自治区清水河县五眼井堡
Wuyanjing Fortress in Qingshuihe County, Inner Mongolia Autonomous Region

山西省偏关县柏羊岭2号堡
Baiyangling No. 2 Fortress in Pianguan County, Shanxi Province

陕西省神木县山峰则堡
Shanfengzebu Fortress, Shenmu
County, Shaanxi Province

陕西省神木县山峰则
堡匾额"卧虎寨"
Inscription Board of
Shanfengzebu Fortress,
Shenmu County, Shaanxi
Province - "Wohuzhai
(Crouching Tiger Fortress)"

陕西省神木县大柏油堡全貌
Full View of Dabaiyoubu Fortress in
Shenmu County, Shaanxi Province

陕西省神木县柏林堡
**Bailinbu Fortress, Shenmu County,
Shaanxi Province**

陕西省神木县高家堡
**Gaojiabu Fortress, Shenmu County,
Shaanxi Province**

陕西省神木县高家堡映北辰台
**Yingbeichentai Watchtower in
Gaojiabu Fortress, Shenmu County,
Shaanxi Province**

1	2
3	

1～3.陕西省榆林市榆阳区易马城堡

Yimacheng (Horse Trading City) Fortress in Yuyang District, Yulin City, Shaanxi Province

宁夏回族自治区灵武市清水营
Qingshuiying Garrison in Lingwu City, Ningxia Hui Autonomous Region

<u>1　2</u>
　3

1.宁夏回族自治区中卫市米粮营子堡
Miliangyingzi Garrison in Zhongwei City, Ningxia Hui Autonomous Region

2.宁夏回族自治区中卫市下滩2号堡
Xiatan No. 2 Fortress in Zhongwei City, Ningxia Hui Autonomous Region

3.宁夏回族自治区同心县周儿庄2号小堡内废弃的营垒
The abandoned barracks in Zhou'erzhuang No. 2 Small Fortress in Tongxin County, Ningxia Hui Autonomous Region

甘肃省靖远县苦水堡
Kushui Fortress in Jingyuan County, Gansu Province

甘肃省民勤县黑山堡
Heishan Fortress in Minqin County, Gansu Province

甘肃省永昌县毛卜喇堡
Maobula Fortress in Yongchang County, Gansu Province

甘肃省山丹县峡口古城过街楼
The Arcade of Xiakou Fortress in Shandan County, Gansu Province

324

甘肃省嘉峪关市野麻湾堡
Yemawan Fortress in Jiayuguan City, Gansu Province

甘肃省嘉峪关关城全景
Full View of Jiayuguan Pass, Gansu Province

甘肃省嘉峪关关城
Jiayuguan Pass, Gansu Province

甘肃省嘉峪关关城光化楼
Guanghua Tower of Jiayuguan Pass, Gansu Province

青海省乐都县孟家湾堡
Mengjiawan Fortress in Ledu County,
Qinghai Province

青海省乐都县碾木沟堡
Nianmugou Fortress in Ledu
County, Qinghai Province

青海省乐都县寺磨庄1号堡
Simozhuang No. 1 Fortress in Ledu
County, Qinghai Province

$$\frac{1}{2\quad 3}$$

1.青海省民和县松树堡
 Songshubao Fortress in Minhe County, Qinghai Province

2.青海省互助县马营堡
Maying Fortress, Huzhu County, Qinghai Province

3.青海省互助县下马圈堡东南角楼
Southeastern Watchtower of Xiamajuan Fortress in Huzhu County, Qinghai Province

青海省大通县平乐堡
Pingle Fortress in Datong County, Qinghai Province

青海省湟中县董家湾堡
Dongjiawan Fortress in Huangzhong County, Qinghai Province

青海省西宁市总寨堡城门楼
Gate Tower of Zongzhai Fortress in Xining City, Qinghai Province

青海省湟中县下脖项关
Xiaboxiangguan Pass, Huangzhong County,
Qinghai Province

青海省门源县老虎沟口关
Laohugoukou Pass, Menyuan County, Qinghai Province

相关遗存
Related Remains

辽宁省绥中县将军石摩崖石刻
Cliff Stone Carvings on Jiangjunshi, Suizhong County, Liaoning Province

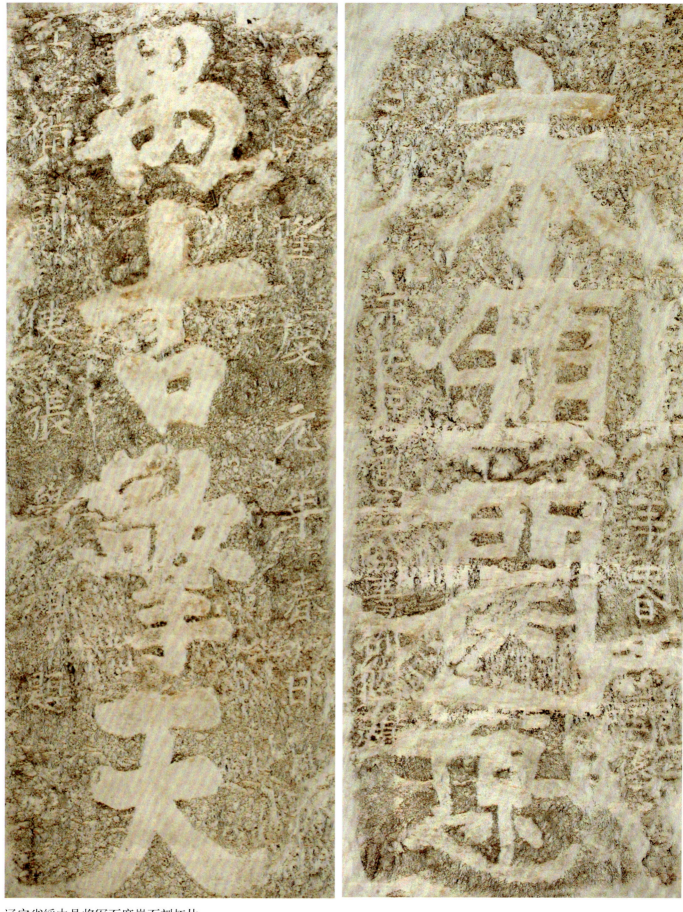

辽宁省绥中县将军石摩崖石刻拓片
Rubbings of Cliff Stone Carvings on Jiangjunshi, Suizhong County, Liaoning Province

河北省秦皇岛市山海关区"天下第一关"匾额
The Inscription Board of "The First Pass under Heaven" in Shanhaiguan District, Qinhuangdao City, Hebei Province

河北省秦皇岛市山海关区11号敌台匾额
The Inscription Board of the No. 11 Watchtower in Shanhaiguan District, Qinhuangdao City, Hebei Province

河北省秦皇岛市山海关区东罗城城墙文字砖
The Inscribed Brick on the Wall of the Eastern Barbican in Shanhaiguan District, Qinhuangdao City, Hebei Province

河北省抚宁县"香山纪寿"石刻
The "Xiangshan Jishou (Congretulation of General Qi Jiguang's Birthday)" Stone Inscription in Funing County, Hebei Province

河北省滦平县金山岭长城文字砖
The Inscribed Brick on Jinshanling Great Wall in Luanping County,
Hebei Province

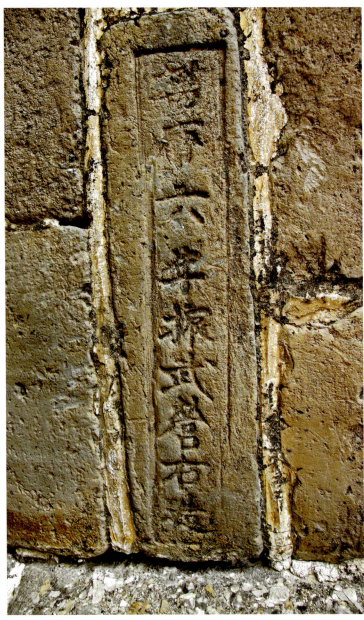

河北省滦平县金山岭长城文字砖
The Inscribed Brick on Jinshanling Great Wall in Luanping
County, Hebei Province

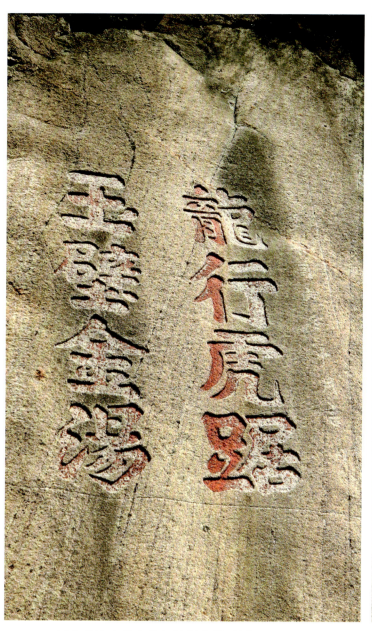

河北省涞水县大龙门城堡摩崖石刻
Cliff Stone Carvings of Dalongmenbao Fortress in Laishui County, Hebei Province

河北省涞水县大龙门城堡摩崖石刻
Cliff Stone Carvings of Dalongmenbao Fortress in Laishui County, Hebei Province

河北省涞水县大龙门城堡摩崖石刻
Cliff Stone Carvings of Dalongmenbu Fortress in Laishui County, Hebei Province

1.河北省涞源县 "插字四十五号台" 匾额

The Inscription Board of "The No. 45 Watchtower of 'Cha' Series" in Laiyuan County, Hebei Province

2.河北省涞源县 "浮字二十九台" 匾额

The Inscription Board of "The No. 29 Watchtower of 'Fu' Series" in Laiyuan County, Hebei Province

河北省抚宁县板场峪砖窑
The Brick Kiln in Banchangyu, Funing County, Hebei Province

河北省抚宁县板场峪砖窑窑门
The Door of the Brick Kiln in Banchangyu, Funing County, Hebei Province

天津市蓟县古强峪寨堡水井
Water Well in Guqiangyu Fortress, Jixian County, Tianjin

天津市蓟县大平安寨堡水井
Water Well in Daping'an Fortress, Jixian County, Tianjin

天津市蓟县中营寨堡四眼水井
Four Wells in Zhongying Fortress, Jixian County, Tianjin

天津市蓟县船舱峪7号烟灶
Smoke Hearth No. 7 of Chuancangyu Great Wall in Jixian County, Tianjin

天津市蓟县青山岭长城2号烟灶
Smoke Hearth No. 2 of Qingshanling Great Wall in Jixian County, Tianjin

天津市蓟县青山岭2号水窖
No. 2 Water Cistern of Qingshanling Great Wall, Jixian County, Tianjin

1 2
3

1.天津市蓟县车道峪长城11号居住址
No. 11 Residential Area of Chedaoyu Great Wall, Jixian County, Tianjin

2.天津市蓟县车道峪长城20号居住址
No. 20 Residential Area of Chedaoyu Great Wall, Jixian County, Tianjin

3.天津市蓟县前干涧长城1号火池
No. 1 Fire Nest of Qianganjian Great Wall, Jixian County, Tianjin

北京市平谷区带便门的登城步道
Mounting Steps of Great Wall with Secret Door in Pinggu
District, Beijing

北京市平谷区长城墙体上的排水设施
The Drainage Facilities on the Great Wall in Pinggu District, Beijing

内蒙古自治区丰镇市隆盛
庄石刻题记
Stone Inscription in
Longshengzhuang Township,
Fengzhen City, Inner Mongolia
Autonomous Region

内蒙古自治区凉城县八敦窑3号挡马墙
No. 3 Stockade in Badunyao, Liangcheng County, Inner Mongolia Autonomous Region

山西省右玉县大同中路分属西界碑
Border tablet indicating the subordination to the western part of Middle Datong Route, Youyu County, Shanxi Province

陕西省榆林市榆阳区红石峡摩崖石刻"雄石峡"及石窟寺
Cliff Stone Carvings of Hongshi Gorge in, Yuyang District Yulin City, Shaanxi Province - "Xiongshi Gorge" and Cave Temple

陕西省榆林市榆阳区红石峡摩崖石刻
Cliff Stone Carvings of Hongshi Gorge in Yuyang District, Yulin City, Shaanxi Province

陕西省榆林市榆阳区红石峡摩崖石刻"长天铁垛"、"华夷天堑"、"襟山带河"

Cliff Stone Carvings of Hongshi Gorge in Yuyang District, Yulin City, Shaanxi Province - "Changtiantieduo", "Huayitianqian" and "Jinshandaihe"

宁夏回族自治区盐池县苠苠沟长城内侧水井
Water Well inside the Jijigou Great Wall, Yanchi County, Ningxia Hui Autonomous Region

宁夏回族自治区灵武市水洞沟长城墙体外侧品字窖
Triangle horse pitfalls outside the Shuidonggou Great Wall, Lingwu City, Ningxia Hui Autonomous Region

甘肃省景泰县索桥堡桥墩遗址（下为黄河）
The Remains of the Bridge Pier of Suoqiaobu Fortress in Jingtai County, Gansu Province (Below is Yellow River)

后 记

　　2005～2006年，国家先后颁布了《"长城保护工程（2005～2014年）"总体工作方案》、《长城保护条例》，开启了"长城保护工程"。

　　作为"长城保护工程"的先导工作，"长城资源调查项目"于2006年正式启动。这是一项由国家主导，多部门、多学科、多单位合作，各级政府积极参与的大型调查项目。经过四年的努力，长城资源调查圆满结束。明长城资源调查，是长城资源调查工作的重要组成部分。《明长城》，便是这次调查的成果之一。

　　《明长城》的编纂工作是在国家文物局的主持下进行的。由国家文物局文物保护与考古司世界遗产处、中国文化遗产研究院长城资源调查工作项目组具体负责组织协调工作。长城沿线十个省、直辖市、自治区文物主管部门分别撰写和选送了本区内的长城调查资料的文字稿和长城照片，形成了本书初稿。在此基础上，文物出版社承担了图片的遴选。初稿文字和图片经国家文物局和中国文化遗产研究院审定。

　　本图录的近600幅长城照片是从长城沿线各省、直辖市、自治区文物工作者亲手拍摄的数十万幅长城图片中挑选出来的。虽说许多照片难以称得上艺术作品，但是每幅照片都是他们努力工作方能获得，饱含了他们对伟大长城的深厚情感。区区数百幅照片难以完整展示万里长城的全貌及其所承载的全部历史和文化信息，但是也足以展示作为世界文化遗产无与伦比的雄伟与壮丽，足以反映长城资源调查工作所取得的巨大成果。

　　由国家文物局主持，中国文化遗产研究院和长城沿线十个省、直辖市、自治区参与编纂的《长城资源调查报告》（综合卷和分省卷）也在陆续编辑出版之中。有关长城的科学、权威的资料信息即将完整、全面地呈现在广大读者面前。

　　长城资源调查是一项规模宏大的文物保护基础性工程。此项工程的实施与完成，与党中央国务院的重视和关怀分不开；与国家文物局各部门的配合分不开；与国家测绘局领导和各级政府部门的大力支持分不开；与长城沿线各省、直辖市、自治区政府的大力支持，各有关部门和单位的通力协作分不开；与中国文化遗产研究院长城资源调查工作项目组和各省长城专家的悉心指导和严格检查监督分不开；更与全国数以万计的文物管理干部和基层文物工作者的辛勤工作分不开！他们以崇高的使命感、强烈的责任心和严谨的科学态度投入到长城资源调查工作之中去，在开展调查工作的一千多个日日夜夜，他们不畏酷暑严寒，翻山越岭，风餐露宿，历尽艰险，足迹踏遍长城沿线的山山水水。为了获得长城的每一个科学数据，他们付出了无数的汗水与艰辛。《明长城》是长城资源调查的具体成果，也是所有参与者辛勤汗水的结晶。

　　在本书出版之际，我们谨向中国文化遗产研究院，向北京市、天津市、辽宁省、内蒙古自治区、河北省、山西省、陕西省、甘肃省、宁夏回族自治区、青海省及其所属各级文物主管部门，向所有参与、支持此项工作的单位、专家和工作人员致以崇高的敬意与感谢！

编　者
2012年6月

Postscript

In 2005 and 2006, the central government issued The General Plan of the Great Wall Protection Project (2005-2014) and The Regulation on the Protection of Great Wall, symbolizing the starting of the Great Wall Protection Project.

As the preparation and the guiding work of the Great Wall Protection Project, the "Great Wall Resource Investigation Project" formally started in 2006. This investigation project is a large-scale investigation run by the state, multi-administration, multidiscipline and multi-institution cooperated and participated in by the governments of all of the levels. Through four years of efforts, the Great Wall Resource Investigation Project is successfully finished. The Ming Great Wall resource investigation is an important part of this project and this Ming Great Wall is the result of this investigation.

The editing work of this Ming Great Wall is supervised by the State Administration of Cultural Heritage. The Cultural Relic and Heritage Bureau of the Cultural Heritage Protection Department of the State Administration of Cultural Heritage and the Great Wall Project Managing Group of the Chinese Academy of Cultural Heritage are in charge of the organization and coordination of the entire project, and the cultural heritage administrations of the ten provinces (municipalities and autonomous regions) through which the Great Wall goes are in charge of the composing of the textural contents and selecting the pictorial materials for this book. The Cultural Relics Press reselected the submitted pictorial materials, and the State Administration of Cultural Heritage and the Chinese Academy of Cultural Heritage reviewed all of the materials to be published in this book.

The more than 600 photographs are selected from the hundreds of thousands of photographs taken by the Great Wall investigators of the ten provinces, municipalities and autonomous regions through which the Great Wall goes. Most of the photographs cannot be considered as "artworks" indeed, but every piece of the image is fetched through their hard work and contains their great feelings to the Great Wall. The few hundred pictures really cannot fully display the spectacle of the Great Wall let alone the historic and cultural information it carries; however, they are able to show the peerless magnificence and marvelousness of the Great Wall as the World Heritage and the great achievements of the Great Wall resource investigation project.

The Great Wall Resource Investigation Reports (provincial volumes) supervised by the State

Administration of Cultural Heritage and compiled by the cultural administrations of the ten provinces (municipalities and autonomous regions) through which the Great Wall goes are also going to be published successively. The scientific and authorized information of the Great Wall will be completely and comprehensively shown to our readers.

The Great Wall resource investigation is a large-scale basic project for cultural heritage protection. The carrying out and fulfillment of this project could not be done without the attention and concern of the Central Committee of the CPC and the State Council, the coordination of various sectors of the State Administration of Cultural Heritage, the support of National Administration of Surveying, Mapping and Geoinformation and the affiliated administrations and institutions, the support and cooperation of the governments and the relevant departments and units of the provinces, municipalities and autonomous regions through which the Great Wall goes, the careful directions and strict supervisions of the experts from the Chinese Academy of Cultural Heritage and the relevant provinces, the hard work of the editors of the Cultural Relics Press; and, above all, the devotion and hard work of the tens of thousands of the cultural heritage protection cadres and workers all over the country! They devoted themselves to the investigation work with their high sense of calling, strong sense of responsibility and rigorous scientific attitude; they braved the severe weathers and the rough paths and left their footprints along the whole Great Wall courses. To fetch every scientific datum, they paid countless sweats and hard work. This book is the concrete result of the Ming Great Wall resource investigation, and also the crystal of the sweats of all of the participants of this project.

At the publishing of this book, please let us pay our acknowledgements and respects to, Chinese Academy of Cultural Heritage, the cultural heritage administrations of Beijing, Tianjin, Liaoning, Inner Mongolia, Hebei, Shanxi, Shaanxi, Gansu, Ningxia and Qinghai, and all of the institutions, experts and colleagues who have participated in and given support to our project!

The Editor